Dual Citizen: The Arrival

Book 3

Tracy Staples-Wilson
and Bob Zuber

Library of Congress Registration Number
TXu 2-141-903
Effective Date of Registration: April 9, 2018

First Edition: Dual Citizen, April 2018
ISBN: 9781642546248

Second Edition: Dual Citizen: The Arrival – Book 3, May 2019
ISBN: 9781097191512
Printed in the United States of America

DEDICATION

The authors thank the following for their invaluable input:

Kate Jakobsen, Kelley Page Jibrell,
Anne Donovan Moran, Lisa Raymond,
and the Tall Shiny Silver Figure:

Hebrews 1:

*[3] Who being the brightness of His glory,
and the express image of His person,
and upholding all things by the word of His power,
when He had by Himself purged our sins,
sat down on the right hand of the Majesty on high:*

*[4] Being made so much better than the angels,
as He hath by inheritance obtained
a more excellent name than they.*

CONTENTS

Ephesians 2:

*¹⁹ Now therefore ye are no more strangers and foreigners,
but fellowcitizens with the saints, and of the household of God;*

*²⁰ And are built upon the foundation of the apostles and prophets,
Jesus Christ himself being the chief corner stone;*

*²¹ In whom all the building fitly framed together
groweth unto an holy temple in the Lord:*

*²² In whom ye also are builded together
for an habitation of God through the Spirit.*

- The King James Bible*

*All verses quoted in this book come from
The King James Bible.

Tracy's Family

Moody: First Name: Kindel, Son of Richard and Emma,
                   Married to Granny, Raised Vera and Jinny,
                   Grandfather to Tracy, Freddie, Mia, Demi and Marie

Granny: First Name: Jackie, Daughter of Granny Berger,
                   Married to Moody, Mother of Vera and Jinny,
                   Grandmother to Tracy, Freddie, Mia, Demi and Marie

Granny Berger: Granny's Mother.

Vera: Oldest Daughter of Granny, Mother of Tracy and
                   Freddie, Married to Big Freddie, then Bobby

Jinny: Second Daughter of Granny, Mother of Mia,
                   Demi and Marie, Married to Squeaky, then Alvin

Freddie: Vera's Second Child, Tracy's younger Brother,
                   Raised with Mia, Demi and Marie

Bobby: Vera's Second Husband, Father of David

Momma Ro: First Name: Rosetta, Married to Charlie,
                   Mother of Tori and Bunky, Vera's Best Friend

Mr. & Mrs. Moody: First Names: Richard and Emma,
                   Parents of Moody and Dris. Tracy's Great Grandfather

Granny Betty: Mother of Squeaky, Granny's Best Friend

Uncle Alvin: Jinny's Third Husband,
                   Raised Tracy's 'Runnin' Cousins' Mia, Demi and Marie

Harry: Tracy's Father, Married to Lynn, Father of Bryan

Lucille: Harry's Mother, Tracy's Paternal Grandmother

Bryan: Tracy's Brother, Son of Harry and Lynn

- Tracy in 'Horse Stance'

Chapter 30

Harry and Lynn welcomed their son into their home, although it was an odd thing for Tracy to live with his parents at his age. Accordingly, Tracy wanted to pay rent and find a job, but his first task was to get Granny to stop calling. She couldn't understand how Tracy could pass by her house.

"Why didn't you come here?" Granny asked. "I've been takin' care of you all my life. You got the key to the house. I raised you. I know you best. Your father don't know you."

Tracy couldn't explain why he was in Columbus, other than God had sent him.

"Watch this," Granny said. "I'll get your room ready, an' I'll make sure he puts you out now. Put your father on the phone," and Tracy did. "Did you know your son was gay?" Granny cackled.

However, Granny already played that card with Harry during the famous car incident after Tracy graduated high school. Still, Harry's countenance became troubled, and he went to his bedroom with the phone to speak with Granny privately. When he came back, he

1

handed the phone to Tracy.

"She's really upset with you son," Harry said, "but she wants to talk with you."

"Well," Granny said. "There was nothin' I could say to put you out of his house. He also said he'd take care of you, an' you were free to go if you wanted to come back."

"I know that Granny," Tracy said. "But for whatever reason, I am supposed to be here."

Moody chimed in from the other phone. "Is God really directin' ya boy? Or are ya just fuckin' up. 'Cause ya know this is crazy."

But Tracy was in Columbus to stay, and he was front and center. Harry and Lynn's home was at the entrance of their well-manicured development. It was a large stucco house with a steep roof for snow, with classical brick columns and a recessed front entryway. The family entered from the side garage, and passed the laundry and two guest rooms into a great room. The kitchen was along the back with a separating island, before white Berber carpet with a rose relief magnified the home's spacious formality. Harry's office was opposite the formal dining room, separated by the front door and hall. Harry and Lynn's bedroom suite took up the other end of the house.

Off the back of the great room was a small Florida room, which led to a patio and grill. Everything was staged over the immense finished basement, which had an informal carpeted living area and fireplace. So the dichotomy of Granny and Moody's house, compared with Harry and Lynn's, couldn't have been clearer. Yet Tracy was both, even without meeting his father's part of himself until his teens, and, according to God, that was why Tracy was in Ohio.

When Tracy returned, his little brother Bryan was in college. So it was just Tracy, Harry and Lynn in the house. But one issue had to be solved, so Harry called Tracy into his office. Unlike Tracy's meetings with Moody, Harry's meetings were more formal. Everything was in its place on Harry's large desk, and his library occupied the wall behind alphabetized by subject.

So, even in a jogging suit, Harry looked ready for a board meeting. The first conference was about the Christian fish decal with rainbow stripes stuck on Tracy's Jeep. The idea of a gay Christian son was an oxymoron to the household at the time. It wasn't something Tracy's parents wanted displayed in their driveway at the entrance of their development. Tracy recognized the roadblock the enemy put in his way. He wasn't going to let any offense hinder him, so he removed the decal.

However, as difficulties mounted, Tracy realized whatever he had to learn about his father's bloodline was important. Dark forces seemed at work from all angles. Another confirmation of this came the following week. Tracy hadn't found a job, and Lynn couldn't understand why.

She was on the kitchen side of the island in the great room. She sipped a juice she made, and Tracy sipped his on the living room side.

"This doesn't make any sense," Lynn said. "Remember how we got your first job?"

"Yes," Tracy said, "and I don't understand this either."

"I mean, I certainly don't mind you being here," Lynn said. "But you just went around the world. It seems strange you're supposed to come back here."

"This is where He told me I need to be," Tracy said.

"Well," Lynn stated. "You are a child of God, and supposed to have shelter and clothing. You're needs are supposed to be met, and the devil is a liar!"

Suddenly, the house shook gently. Tracy simultaneously broke into a cold sweat, but like someone had dropped a bucket of water over his head, to the point Tracy felt water well up in his shoes. Harry felt the tremor, ran from his office, and was uncharacteristically hyper.

"Is Tracy working out?" Harry asked, and then Harry saw Tracy.

"If that wasn't you, what was that shaking?" and then Harry noticed Tracy was wet, and looked at Lynn. "What did you do? Did you spray him with water?"

Lynn shot her husband a penetrating look, but Tracy was completely doused.

"Why are you wet Tracy?" Harry asked. "Did you just exercise or something?"

"No Dad," Tracy said. "This is the first time He has ever done this."

Soon after, Tracy got a job that included travel during the week, and things settled into a routine. Tracy also enjoyed being back at Christian Assembly. The congregation was gearing up for a symposium over the Fourth of July holiday. Through their conversations about church, Harry was pleasantly surprised how much Tracy knew of the church and scripture. Harry also began to wonder about his son's relationship with God.

At the same time, Harry was uneasy with Tracy's public acknowledgement of this relationship. Harry and Lynn were both concerned how a man of God should be seen in the world. For instance, one evening, Tracy came out from his room and headed out. Lynn saw his red sneakers and shot Harry a look.

Before Tracy realized it, Harry jumped off the couch, and somehow beat Tracy to the front door. The only time Tracy saw his father move faster was during a previous summer visit. Harry came home and saw Tracy on the front steps. After he parked his Cadillac in the garage, Harry came through the house. Then he opened and closed the front door to see what was so interesting.

"Son," Harry said. "What are you doing?"

"It's fascinating Dad," Tracy said. "I'm watching this garden snake stalk this frog."

"Snake!?!" Harry shouted. "You got to kill that thing!"

By the time Tracy looked up, Harry stood behind him with a snow shovel. He had run to the garage to get it, and returned before

Tracy had moved. In fact, the door alarm hadn't finished beeping from the door being reopened, and Tracy began to laugh.

"It's not funny son," Harry said, a little out of breath.

"A snow shovel Dad?" Tracy asked.

"It's the biggest thing I could find," Harry said quickly. "Now kill it!" So, Moody wasn't the only patriarch to have a snake as his kryptonite. Now, Harry managed to pass Tracy to block his exit in his very red sneakers.

"Son," Harry said sweetly. "Where are you going?" and Harry leaned awkwardly on the wall with his elbow to block the door. Although, Harry's pose made it look like he was about to get a cramp in his ankle.

"I'm going to the movies Dad," Tracy answered.

"Dressed like that?"

"What's wrong Dad?"

"Those shoes," Harry said gently. "You are going out of the house in those shoes?"

"These are my most comfortable chucks Dad."

"But, they are red son."

"So?"

"Well," Harry decided. "Your Mom and I have decided that I need to take you shopping."

"Ok," because Tracy still didn't understand.

"But, in the mean time, do you have some penny loafers or something?"

"Sure Dad, I can do that," and Tracy changed his shoes.

But their shoes represented the divide: Tracy's red sneakers, and his father's pristine dress shoes. Harry's walk with God ended up with him being a public figure as a teacher and minister. His house anchored his community, his ministry fortified his church, and Harry routinely ran into previous high school students and their growing families at the grocery store. Tracy's path took him through the southern desert, made him a cool corporate consultant, and his red sneakers had actually gone to gay bars where he watched drag performances of Kristy MacColl's song, "In these Shoes?"

To narrow the disparity Harry and Tracy went shopping, and Lynn wasn't the only one who loved clothes. Harry's passion not only made him a snappy dresser, there was a purpose. His dress shirts were pressed to perfection, and his first, middle and last name was embroidered on the right sleeve, which was revealed when Harry shook someone's hand. But that wasn't the only thing. When Tracy picked a polo shirt off a sale rack, Harry grimaced.

"Son," Harry said. "Let me show you something," and Harry reluctantly took the polo to hold it for Tracy. "Here son, feel the edge of this sleeve," and Tracy did. "This fabric will cut you."

Harry discarded the offending fabric, and grabbed an exquisite polo from a hanger behind him. "Try this one," Harry said proudly. "See, this is what you want. Something that will love you back."

So Tracy learned a few tricks, but his style was pretty much set by this time. Left to his own devices, Tracy went back to his casual ways. Later, at the grocery store, Tracy stood next to his father in the juice aisle, deciding.

"Ok Lord," Tracy said. "What's better for me after a workout - coconut water, or aloe vera juice?"

"Son," Harry said. "You could say that to the Lord silently."

"Muzzle the ox, and you will not get the results," He said. *"If you do not say it, you will not see it."*

Tracy looked at his father and wondered if he heard anything, but Harry moved on to the fresh fruit department.

"See what Lord?" Tracy said softly.

*"Remember? 'Man shall not live by bread alone, but by **every** word that proceedeth out of the mouth of God.' I am a builder. Everything that comes out of My mouth is meant to expand and cause increase. So if you do not speak our conversations out loud, there will not be a manifestation in the earth. If you just 'think' our conversation, the only thing you will receive from Me are dreams and visions. Building manifestations starts by speaking My conversations out loud."*

7

"That's pretty cool Lord," Tracy said.

"If you act like I am real, than I will be real to you. If you keep Me in your mind, that is where I will stay. If you speak our conversations out loud, I will manifest out loud, and you will live life out loud. Live Life Out Loud Tracy."

"Amen!" Tracy shouted, which to Tracy felt great. But Harry was startled by his son's outburst, and looked at Tracy before he picked out the perfect box of strawberries.

Then, the Jubilee at their church was upon them. Tracy went with Harry to pick up one of the guest preachers from the airport. He was a finely dressed black man with alarmingly welcoming eyes, and had a charming English accent mixed with the Caribbean. He and Harry might have been mistaken for brothers except for the preacher's distinct, 1970's-looking clipped beard and connected moustache. When Harry got out of the car, they hugged and called each another brother anyway. The preacher's wife was impeccably dressed, had rich almond colored skin, and an easy smile. Tracy came for their luggage and put it in the trunk of the Cadillac.

"And who is this?" the preacher asked.

"This is my son Tracy," Harry said proudly. "Tracy, this is…"

"Dr. Myles Monroe," Tracy interrupted, and Harry was surprised.

"You follow Dr. Monroe?" Harry asked.

"Please, call me Myles," the preacher said.

Later, after they dropped the Monroes at their hotel, Harry was curious. "You follow Myles?" Harry asked.

"I don't really do anything but watch Christian television when I'm at home," which made Harry ponder his son. "All I know is," Tracy explained, "I am supposed to get more of Him and His word, and that's how I've been able to hold on."

During the festival, Harry and Tracy ferried the Monroes to and from the church. After the last revival, Harry drove the Monroes to the airport with Tracy as co-pilot. Myles sat behind Harry, and his wife Ruth sat behind Tracy in the back seat. They were quiet after so much church, until Dr. Monroe had to speak. His discourse was measurably Bahamian, but he wasn't the one with the message.

"Harry," Myles said, "The Holy Ghost is telling me there is something special about your son. There is a special anointing on him. Did you know that?"

Harry didn't answer.

"Is he your first-born?" Myles asked.

"Why, yes he is," Harry answered.

"Tracy," Myles said. "The Lord is telling me to sow a seed into your life. Harry, would you like to participate in this seed-sowing?"

Harry remained silent. Lynn said Harry was suspicious, which made him 'delayed' sometimes. Ironically, his son was the same way. Both Harry and Tracy liked to test the Spirit to make sure it wasn't a lie from the pit of hell. One of Tracy's favorite sports was procrastination, which, now seemed likely was inherited.

"Nevertheless," Myles said, "I shall sow it myself. Ruth, can you reach one of my books?" and Ruth pulled a book from their carry-on. "Oh," Myles said gently. "Not that one, the other one."

Ruth pulled out a different book with an eagle on the front jacket. Myles opened it, took a pen from his blazer and wrote: 'To: Tracy, May your vision be expanded by this book. God bless you. Love, Uncle Myles, Phil: 1:6.' After he closed the book, Myles held it purposefully. Then, he tapped Tracy on the shoulder with the book three times. Tracy thought Myles was trying to get his attention, but he already had his attention.

"No Tracy," He said. *"He is from the Bahamas, so he understands the English ways of kingdom and duty. He is knighting you with a title."*

'That's odd,' Tracy thought. 'We're in America. What good is a title going to do me in the middle of Ohio?' and then Dr. Monroe confirmed what Tracy just heard.

"I give you a title I have only given three other times before," Myles said, and his wife gasped hard enough to necessitate putting her hands over her mouth. "Read it when you get home," Myles said, "and study it."

As Tracy tried to figure out the spiritual significance of what was going on, Mrs. Monroe leaned up to speak in Tracy's ear.

"You are our nephew," Ruth explained. "That is the title."

When they got home, Tracy looked up Phillipians 1:6 inscribed in his book:

"Being confident of this very thing, that he which hath begun a good work in you will perform it until the day of Jesus Christ:"

To Tracy, the colon at end of the scripture said it all. Tracy still didn't know why he was in Columbus, and his father didn't seem to know why either. A week later, Harry had to go to West Virginia, because his Uncle Bob needed help fixing his plumbing. Harry asked Tracy if he wanted to go. He thought Tracy could visit with Granny and Moody for the weekend, which might calm things. On the road, the two were mostly quiet. Tracy thought about what Uncle Myles had said, and why he was sent to Ohio. Then, he was interrupted.

"Dad," Tracy said. "He's telling me to tell you this: Isn't it odd that we didn't meet until I was fifteen years old?"

Harry was caught off guard.

"Isn't it also peculiar," Tracy said, "that I have the same hand gestures, vocal pattern, and I laugh just like you do? Dad, He is telling me to tell you there is nothing that is a coincidence in Him. We have to figure this thing out in order for me to move forward."

"Ok son," Harry said. "What do you want to know?"

"Well," Tracy said. "I don't know. All He said was, in order for me to move forward, I have to learn and understand the family bloodline," and Tracy paused. "He also says that only you can tell that to me."

When they got to Charleston, Harry dropped Tracy off at Starling Drive. After their hug Granny's face fell to neutral, Moody wheeled himself into the kitchen, and the three had a pow-wow.

"Granny," Tracy said, "believe me, I'm doing what the Lord told me to do."

"Whataya mean?" Granny said.

"If I tell you," Tracy said, "do you promise not to be upset?" and Moody chuckled.

"Ya know me better than that," Granny said. "Out with it."

"Well," Tracy said. "I got a key to your house, an' I don't even have to call you."

Granny relaxed a little, "Yeah…"

"I'm there because God told me to go." Tracy said. "I told Him I didn't want to go, but that's where He sent me, an' I'm paying my own way. I have a job I know is temporary, an' God tells me I'm only supposed to be there until I learn the family bloodline."

"Well," Granny said. "I don't know what that might be, but ya better get to learnin' pretty fast. I don't like the idea of you payin' when you can stay here for free. Shit."

"Aw hell Jackie," Moody snarled. "Let's see how this works out. We got your back boy," and Moody was convinced.

It made sense to Moody that Tracy's connection with the Tall Shiny Silver Figure would come from his father. When Harry and Tracy got back from West Virginia, Tracy got another directive. He knocked on the doorframe to Harry's office, and once Harry looked up from his work, Tracy came in and sat down.

"Hey Dad," Tracy said. "I'm getting ready to do this travel. I'll be away for a few weeks, and God is telling me to ask you the proper way to do communion."

"Why is God asking you to do that son?" Harry asked.

"He wants me to do it every evening while I'm gone. So, if you can show me how to do it, I'll make sure I'm doing it right," and Tracy paused before he added, "He has never told me to do this before."

"You are coming up with the strangest things Tracy."

"I'm not coming up with them, He is. A lot of what He says doesn't make any sense - I just do it. He made me read Psalm 91 every morning for a year before I came here, and that didn't make any sense."

That statement made Harry lean back into his tall leather chair, and look off into the distance.

"Listen son," Harry said. "Your mother called me up shortly after you were three years old. You had just gotten out of the hospital with the high temperature. She told me you were talking to an imaginary friend. She asked me if she should be alarmed, and I told her no. Then I wanted to know if your imaginary friend had a name."

Tracy was surprised. This was the first time Tracy heard his parents had discussed anything about him, especially about the Tall Shiny Silver Figure.

"Well, she couldn't tell me," Harry siad. "Is this the same 'he'," and Harry paused. "Is this the same 'He' you've been talking to?"

"Yes Dad," Tracy said.

"Son, let me tell you something," and his father leaned forward and clasped his hands. "You can't be running around telling people you hear from the Holy Ghost like you do," and Harry's eyebrows went up. "They'll lock you up, and think you're crazy."

Tracy was dumbfounded. Of course, this warning made sense from the 'guns an' hound dogs' point of view when he was three. Or when he painted the vision in the sixth grade, and his class ended up doing 'the snake'. But Tracy had told lots of people in his adult life. Tracy told them how He had gotten him his jobs, helped him do his jobs, find new ones, and his co-workers believed. So at present, his father's warning rang hollow.

"Dad," Tracy said. "I really do talk to Him, and He really does talk back. I can't explain it. That's why I'm here, remember?" and now it was Harry who didn't know what to say. "You're supposed to help me figure this thing out."

"Well son, it seems to me you can't be telling people you hear from God that often. That would mean you hear from God more than Moses did," and Harry was gentle. "Now, are you saying you are greater than Moses?"

Instantly, Tracy felt the Tall Shiny Silver Figure push him aside. It was more powerful than when He took possession of Tracy's arm to make the mountain 'flow like wheatgrass'. This felt like when Tracy went to the funeral home, and the clerk wouldn't let him in to see his mother's body. Then, He said '*I am the first-born,*' and the poor woman had to bow and back her way to unlock the sanctuary door. Like then, Tracy watched the words come from his own mouth, and Tracy felt His righteousness:

"Moses' sacrifice was that of doves, goats and bulls. My covenant is of the precious Blood of Jesus Christ, and I have a right to hear from my Daddy God more than Moses ever did."

Then, Tracy was pushed back into his body, and was just as shocked as Harry. Tracy looked at his father with bewilderment.

"Dad," Tracy said meekly. "That wasn't me that just said that. I don't even know what that means. Do you know what that means?"

Because of his astonishment, Harry spoke even more slowly. "It means I have a lot of work to do, and I have to put together an entirely new message for Sunday."

Chapter 31

- a bamboo forest

By November of 2003, Tracy had been living in Columbus with Harry and Lynn for six months. He hadn't found out what God wanted him to know, and as the days grew shorter and colder, darkness closed in. At the time, Tracy worked with an accounting firm that did Oracle assessments.

Shortly before Thanksgiving, Tracy's supervisor lied to a client about what the company could do for them. When Tracy traveled to the job, he found himself in a situation that would compromise his integrity, and that Tracy's supervisor thought he would go along with it. Instead, Tracy told the client the truth and quit his job, and there were other demons at work behind the scenes.

Tracy spent Christmas and New Years in West Virginia, sipped apricot moonshine, and groused with Moody. When Tracy returned to Columbus, he got another contract he knew was place holding, and winter deepened. To Tracy, an antagonistic attitude grew along with the piles of snow. No one seemed to understand him, and Tracy's frustration was held captive to whatever reason he was supposed be in his father's house. The chill of the endless gray days wore on him, and, by the end of January, Tracy was incensed with God.

"Ok Lord," Tracy said. "I've been here nine months. If a woman can birth something in the natural in nine months, surely You can birth something in the supernatural in the same amount of time."

There was no answer.

"Now, I'm not trying to put a time limit on this, but my parents are also men and women of God. I'm tired of leaning on them, so You need to birth this thing fast."

More time passed, and nothing happened. Nothing was unveiled other than Lynn's frenzied preparations for Harry's surprise birthday party. Finally, on the last Sunday of January, Tracy and Lynn went to Pier One to get finishing flourishes for Harry's party. Tracy smelled a biscotti candle as He spoke.

"Repeat after Me," He said. *"Thank you Father, for my perfect job, my perfect house, my perfect body, and my perfect spouse."*

Because he was angry, Tracy replaced the candle on the shelf before he answered.

"After months of not speaking to me," Tracy said aloud. "You choose Pier One?"

Lynn turned around at the end of the aisle. "Did you find something?"

Tracy was too upset to hear her, the store went away, and it was just he and God who had it out.

"I just sat in church for two hours," Tracy griped, "and spoke to You every night for weeks."

"Who are you talking to Tracy?" Lynn asked.

She now stood next to him, but Tracy didn't see her. He continued as if he was by himself, paced, and spoke a little lower than a yell, which made Lynn look around to see if anyone else noticed.

"We were just in church," and Tracy was sarcastic. "You could have come down with a choir of angels to tell me this. The whole congregation would have gasped and adored You. Or, You could have sent that annoying angel with the clipboard but no, You choose Pier One?"

"Are you done?" He asked.

"I don't wanna be," Tracy said defiantly, "but I am."

"Repeat after Me," He said again. *"Thank you Father, for my perfect job, my perfect house, my perfect body, and my perfect spouse,"* and Tracy obeyed, albeit grudgingly.

"Thank you Father," Tracy repeated aloud. "For my perfect job, my perfect house, my perfect body, and my perfect spouse."

"Good," He said. *"Add that to your prayers."*

"What does that mean," Lynn asked. "Spouse?"

Tracy realized she stood in front of him, but ignored her for a moment. Instead, Tracy repeated the prayer again to make sure he had it, but softly and to himself:

"Thank you Father, for my perfect job, my perfect house, my perfect body, and my perfect spouse," and Lynn was stunned into her Georgia accent.

"Well I ain't never seen nothin' like that before," she said loud enough to turn a few heads. "Seen it plenty-a-times in a church pew. I even fell out a few times in the aisle myself. But I never seen the Lord speak out here in the open. Shoo!"

A week later was the first Sunday of February, and Pastor Sam had an unusual sermon. Tracy had been a member of the youth group since he first attended in 1981. Pastor Sam was an unassuming man, who ended up serving Christian Assembly for forty-one years. He had a high forehead, nicely combed hair, and a plump face that always seemed to be smiling, even when he preached on serious topics.

"Good morning everyone," Pastor Sam said.

"Good morning!" the large congregation said. They were many faiths, although primarily from the Christian and Jewish traditions, as were Pastor Sam and his wife.

"I realize this may not be what you expect this morning," Pastor Sam said. "But I am going to do what the Lord told me to do," and Pastor Sam took his seat.

The congregation stayed quiet for a moment, and wondered whether he was going to preach. Then, Pastor Sam spoke loudly from his seated position.

"For the Lord is good, and His mercy endureth for ever," Pastor Sam stated.

The congregation waited.

"For the Lord is good, and His mercy endureth for ever," Pastor Sam said again, and a few joined him for the end of the phrase. More joined on the next repetition, until the entire congregation stated the confession in unison: "For Lord is good, and His mercy endureth forever!"

After fifteen minutes of the mantra, praise broke out in the church for the next hour, and the service was done. That night, Pastor Sam held a super bowl party for members of Tracy's youth group because a prophecy had come true. Before Tracy returned to Columbus in 2003, it was prophesied the children would come home. Tracy was the first, and many of Tracy's generation followed. Some were finally out of college, or had finished their master's degrees. Others had moved away, but for one reason or another, they came home to live with their parents. Pastor Sam and his wife were sensitive to this, and hosted a super bowl party at their house. Tracy went early to meet with Pastor Sam and vented.

"Why am I stuck here?" Tracy asked. "All He said was, my father is supposed to tell me about the family bloodline. Instead, they look at me like I have three heads, which I feel like I have. I'm not used to this. I've been on my own for years. Granny and Moody could use the help, especially Moody with his wheelchair, rather than being a bother to Mom and Dad here. With my experience, I can find a job pretty much anywhere. I just want to move on. Why does God have me here?"

Pastor Sam looked at Tracy. Then he picked up his Bible from his desk. He flipped through to Psalm 27:10 and read it to himself. Then he set the Bible down and left it open.

"From my experience," Pastor Sam said, "I can't move on until I've done the last thing he told me to do. Now usually, I am the one delaying God, but this is a little tricky because it involves your Dad."

"Why can't God just tell me himself?" Tracy said. "He tells me everything else."

"I am sure He has a reason," Pastor Sam said. "But see if this helps," and he picked up his Bible and read:

"When my father and my mother forsake me, then the Lord will take me up."

Tracy was comforted a little by the scripture, even though Harry and Lynn hadn't forsaken him. Then, at the party the youth group played a game before the super bowl, and things started to move.

"If you could be any tree in the forest," Pastor Sam asked, "what kind would you be, and why."

Some decided to be an oak for strength. Others were apple or peach trees for the fruit they would bear. After a while, Pastor Sam asked Tracy directly.

"I'd be a forest of bamboo," Tracy said decisively.

"Why bamboo?" Pastor Sam asked.

"After you plant it," Tracy explained, "it takes ten years before you see anything, because the roots grow unseen. Finally, when the shoots appear, they can grow three feet in a single day. Even if you cut it down, another, stronger trunk shoots up behind you. The roots are so deep and well-connected, nothing can stop them."

Pastor Sam smiled. A few nights later, Tracy heard Him in a vision.

"Give Me forty-nine, and I will give you fifty," He said.

"But Lord," Tracy said. "I have a fifty dollar bill, just take it all."

"No," He said. *"I just want you to give Me the forty-nine. I do not want you to do anything for the fifty."*

Tracy had no idea what that meant, but was glad He finally heard Him.

The following Sunday was Harry's sixtieth birthday. The surprise Lynn had been planning since Tracy arrived was about to be revealed, and the whole church was involved. Before the party, and for secrecy, Tracy and Bryan went to pick up a dark black man from Barbados, and a lovely blond white woman from England. They were the main surprise for Harry's birthday, and were great faith friends of his father's. The couple introduced themselves when Tracy and Bryan picked them up at the hotel.

"But you must call us Uncle Peter and Aunt Melody," Peter said. "After all, you are Harry's sons!"

Harry's birthday party was a great success. Then, for the next week, Peter and Melody had a great visit with Tracy's parents. Tracy had to work, but he came home early in order to glean as much as possible from Harry's guests. Melody was a prophetess in the church. She saw Tracy spiritually, and both Peter and Melody were practical about God - like farmers who pushed seed into the ground. Tracy had never seen God's word used in such a way, and Peter and Melody were just as fascinated with Tracy.

Like her name, everything about Melody was sing-songy and bright. Peter was cheerfully British, even though he was from the Caribbean. He spoke about everything from being angry with God, to casual discussions of the bliss of marital sex, which made Lynn blush. After dinner one night, Melody said she talked with God all the time, just like He was standing beside her.

"I know people think it's odd," Melody sang, "when I'm carrying on, seemingly by myself as I ride the Tube. But that's how I hear back from Him."

"So, that's what He meant," Tracy said.

Melody looked at Tracy with a smile. "That's right," she coaxed. "Tell us…"

"Muzzle the ox," Tracy repeated, "and you won't get results."

"That's it," Peter said. "First Timothy, Five."

Melody immediately looked it up and read it aloud:

"For the scripture saith, thou shalt not muzzle the ox that treadeth out the corn. And, The labourer is worthy of his reward."

Melody closed her Bible, held it close to her, and looked at the ceiling. "Our words simply fall to the ground," Melody stated. "But every living thing can feed off of us if we speak His word, and send it out into this world."

This statement made Tracy remember the last thing He said to him. Everyone was quiet, and Tracy's expression caught the attention of the room. His eyes grew more golden, and his smile couldn't be hidden.

"Just last week," Tracy said, "He spoke to me in a dream," and Melody was transfixed as Tracy sent His word out. "He said, 'Give Me forty-nine, and I will give you fifty'," and Melody got terribly excited.

"There is only one place in the Bible that forty-nine and fifty are mentioned," she said, "and it speaks about the Jubilee!" Melody opened her Bible to look up Leviticus 25, and was so exuberant she could barely breathe.

"It's right here," and Melody stopped on the page. "God is talking to Moses."

Harry's ears perked up at the mention of Moses, and was reminded of the conversation about the bulls and goats he had with Tracy as Melody read the text:

⁸ And thou shalt number seven sabbaths of years unto thee, seven times seven years; and the space of the seven sabbaths of years shall be unto thee forty and nine years.

⁹ Then shalt thou cause the trumpet of the jubile to sound on the tenth day of the seventh month, in the day of atonement shall ye make the trumpet sound throughout all your land.

¹⁰ And ye shall hallow the fiftieth year, and proclaim liberty throughout all the land unto all the inhabitants thereof: it shall be a jubile unto you; and ye shall return every man unto his possession, and ye shall return every man unto his family."

Then Melody looked at Tracy. "God's going to restore everything you lost Tracy," and she began dancing, "and He's going to make everybody see it!"

Everyone in the house was stopped except the prophetess. Melody frolicked over and handed her Bible to Lynn, who took it to read the whole chapter. Then Melody went and took Tracy by the hand.

"Would you like to go for a walk?" Melody asked gaily, and swung Tracy's hand.

"Sure," Tracy said, and Melody looked at Peter.

Melody and Tracy left for the garage, put on their coats, and walked the circle of the development. Peter came and sat down at the breakfast bar with Harry.

"Tracy told us God told him to come here," Peter said. "We think, well, Melody especially, is hearing we need to find out what he needs, and not delay his progress any further," and Harry looked at Peter.

"I think I know what this is all about now," Harry said. "I will speak with him."

The next day, Melody and Peter left for England. That evening, Harry called Tracy in for what would be the last meeting in his office.

"Uncle Peter and Aunt Melody seem to think you are here for a specific reason," Harry said, and Tracy listened. "Ok," Harry said and exhaled. "This is how it goes…

My grandfather was called into the ministry. His name was Benjamin, and the Lord told him there would be someone following him in the ministry. I was too young to realize he was talking about me. At that time, my grandfather said, 'Lord, if this is you, bless my first-born.'

God's reply was, *'Not only will I bless your first-born with a double portion experience more than what you have, I will perpetuate it. I will give a double portion experience of Me to every first-born in the following generations.'*

So my grandfather was able to hear and talk to God. His first-born was able to hear and talk to God, and do creative miracles. That was my mother, your grandmother, Lucille. One of my first experiences was when I was in college, and I came home to visit. Your grandmother always lived in Vandalia. It was a three-hour drive, and it got late. But I had to drive back to go to work in the morning. I must have left out close to ten-o'clock. So my mother prayed for me before she went to bed. An hour later she awoke, and the next morning she called me.

'How was your trip?' she asked.

I said it was fine, because I didn't want her to know I had fallen asleep at the wheel.

'Well I was wakened, because I saw your car cross the yellow line in the road,' Mother said. 'So I stayed up all night praying in tongues.'

Then I told my mother the truth. I told her I remembered falling asleep, but I didn't remember the last hour-and-a-half of my trip. When I woke up I was in my car, and the car was parked in my driveway with the motor running," and Harry stopped a moment, remembering.

"I know that may not sound like much," Harry said. "But then, Mother told me about the family blessing when I was old enough. I must have been thirteen. No, I was older, maybe fifteen."

"That's how old I was when I met you," Tracy said.

"My," Harry said. "Yes it was. How about that. Well, Mother told me what I just told you, about her father and the family blessing, and then she showed me. My mother had five sisters, and they had a prayer meeting at the house on a Saturday night. Early Sunday morning, I heard my mother and her sister in the dining room praying in the Holy Ghost. That wasn't unusual, but there was a little girl who sat in one of the dining room chairs. She was the daughter of a friend of one of my Aunts. Everyone knew she had one leg that was bigger than the other, and she walked with a limp. When I came out of my bedroom, I could tell this wasn't a normal prayer. When she saw me, my mother turned to me, and the Lord spoke through her:

'This is a witness for thy son.'

Then she and my Aunt began praying in tongues again. They laid their hands on her big leg, and as they prayed the little girl's leg shrunk down to its normal size. I saw it happen."

Harry paused again, because the miracle was as fresh to him as when it happened.

"Afterward she got up, and went home without a limp," and Harry smiled. "Then I ran to the church and got myself straightened out, and I've been there ever since."

Then Harry looked at his son sweetly. "Your grandmother prayed for you a lot," he said.

"I wouldn't have known that," Tracy said. "I remember seeing her when I was little, at that intersection. Mom yelled at her, and she pulled out like a bat out of hell."

"Well son," and Harry's eyebrow went up. "I think your mother surprised her," and he bent his head forward, "but I heard about that."

"It sounds like you were around behind the scenes, I just never saw you," Tracy said.

"I stayed away," Harry said. "Your other Granny made sure of that, but I was around. I kept my distance until you were old enough to search me out, and I knew you would."

"And now I'm here to search out the bloodline," Tracy said, but then he wanted a clarification. "Do you hear Him, I mean, like I do?"

Harry looked at his son and thought a moment. "Probably not as often, by the sounds of it. But yes, I hear Him. Like when my wife wanted to build this house," and they both laughed. "I was getting ready to retire. I didn't want to build a new house, but your mother was all about it."

Tracy remembered all the strife that went into the real cherry wood cabinets for the kitchen during construction of the house.

Then Harry continued.

"So I fought against it and got angry at God," Harry admitted. "I couldn't understand why we needed a new house, and I went into a bookstore at the mall. He said, *'I am leading,'* and then I was overpowered to the point I began weeping."

Harry looked at Tracy, smiled, shrugged his shoulders and held up his hands. "And that was that. Once I recovered and gave it over to Him, there was our house on the cover of a magazine. The contractors fell into place and before I knew it, the house was built and we were living in it."

"That all sounds familiar," Tracy said. "I snot and cry at God all the time. Once I stop, He asks me if I'm done," and Harry laughed with his son. "Then He makes it plain, once I get out of the way."

"Hmm," Harry mused, and had another revelation.

"But it sounds like there's more," Tracy said.

"There is," Harry said, and began to understand why this conversation was important. "The house was a small thing really, and there is a reason my ministry is with the elderly."

Tracy didn't understand.

"You see," Harry said. "Lucille's blessing was creative miracles, like when she healed the girl with the big leg. But there was more…

When Ben died, my grandfather, he was in the living room sitting in his chair. Ben had been dead for a while and my grandmother, Lily, was praying over him, so we stayed with her. Then she was overcome with grief and asked the Lord, 'Let me speak with him one more time.'

Ben rose up and said, 'It's alright Lily,' and he fell back again into his chair."

Then, the first-born of the third and fourth generations took in that moment of the blessing.

"Now," Harry continued. "I was in Columbus when my mother Lucille died. She was fairly young at age sixty-two, and went into the hospital for a routine surgery. The night before she died her nurse called the family in, but I was in Columbus. The nurse called in the morning to say she had gone, and that they would leave the body in the room until I got there. When I did, I went to the window to pray. I thought of my grandmother, and what happened with Ben after he died, but the Lord interrupted me.

'She does not want to come back,' He said. Then Mother's nurse came in to confirm this. She told me how tired Lucille was, and that she didn't want to come back, and I understood. But all of this makes me think about what Lily said."

"What do you mean Dad?" Tracy asked.

"My grandmother only asked to speak with my grandfather one more time," and Harry's eyebrows went up. "What if Lily had asked for more? What if she asked for a year?"

"Or his youth to be renewed," Tracy said.

"Exactly son," Harry said, "which makes me wonder what you will do," and Tracy smiled at his Dad, and was at peace.

Selah.

Chapter 32

- at the river

Tracy was at the river behind Granny and Moody's house. It was a beautiful summer day. He sat on his haunches on the shore, and picked up rocks and threw them in the water. When Tracy looked down the river, he saw a man walking on the water. He had on a shiny robe, and Tracy recognized Him to be the Lord. He was in His human form, called Jesus, in order to show what Tracy could do within his own human form.

When Tracy saw Him as the Tall Shiny Silver Figure, He was Elohim - all God - the created One. At those times He was all light, nothing could stop Him, and everything belonged to Him. Now, Jesus walked in the middle of the river, but He wasn't walking toward Tracy. His path was down the middle. He looked at Tracy, although He didn't say anything. In fact, the Lord appeared not to pay Tracy too much mind.

Tracy thought, 'Hey, I've got enough experience in these visions to recognize I can ask for some stuff – 'you have not because you ask not'.'

Tracy wasn't afraid because it was peaceful. But this also wasn't the Tall Shiny Silver Figure - the jovial 'imaginary friend' from when he was three. This was Jesus, a grown man like himself, which made Tracy reluctant. Tracy didn't want to step out of the boat only to sink. Instead, Tracy tried to think of something Peter didn't think of in the storm, and then he was encouraged.

"Give a man a fish, and he will go hungry the next day," the Holy Ghost said. *"Teach him how to fish, and he could earn his own living, and have his own business."*

By this time, Jesus was adjacent to Tracy, and Tracy realized the Lord would keep going if he didn't say anything. Tracy also understood the Lord must be recognized, and His goodness must be acknowledged. So Tracy mustered his faith as Jesus passed him.

"Hey," Tracy said, and waved.

Jesus stopped and looked, because He was hoping Tracy would say something.

"Show me how you do that," Tracy said.

Jesus was impressed with Tracy's words. Jesus could teach from a distance, as a lecturer does in front of a chalkboard, or from a boat before a crowd. However, Jesus' preferred method of teaching was being present with a student, so He could show them how to do something. That way, the lesson would be understood by experience and could never be taken away.

"Come on," Jesus said.

At Tracy's first gesture to get up from his haunches to obey, he immediately stood in front of Jesus in the middle of the river. Tracy wondered how he got there so fast, but he didn't get distracted. Tracy kept his eyes fixed on His as they walked down the river. And the Lord's face was a beautiful outline of His human form in light – His beard, His warm smile and flowing hair.

But His eyes were a flame – literally, like the flame a common lighter produced. Tracy wanted to ask, but his thought was interrupted.

"That is a different lesson," Jesus said kindly, "which I believe you already know," and Jesus looked at Tracy with a knowing glance. "I believe He already told you," and Tracy knew the 'He' Jesus referred to was the Holy Ghost. "He can't keep a secret."

Tracy thought Jesus was funny and 'had serious jokes', which helped him relax. However, Tracy was still walking with Him down the middle of the river on water, so he didn't take his eyes from Jesus' face. As they walked, Tracy knew they went where the Lord had been, and the path was where Tracy was headed. Jesus had walked this path earlier, to make sure it was secure before He came back to get Tracy. After this revelation, Tracy was emboldened, but he still didn't take his eyes off the Lord's.

"Lord," Tracy said. "This is good and all, but I asked you to show me how you do this."

"Ok," He said. "Look down."

"Oh no," Tracy said. "Not me. That's how You got the last one," and Tracy laughed, referring to Peter.

"And You know how I feel about "Jaws", and how I can't put my hands in soapy dishwater, and You want me to look down?"

"No really," He said. "Look down."

"Are you sure I'm not going to sink?"

"Really Tracy," and He said it a third time: "Look down."

Tracy looked. Under his feet was a series of stone columns that weren't connected. As Tracy walked, a single column of stone rose to meet his foot. Each column stopped just below the surface of the water, so only the soles of Tracy's shoes got wet. The pillars couldn't be seen from shore, but they were always out there in the deep, waiting to be called.

Tracy was made to understand he walked on stones of revelation knowledge, which were built through praying in the spirit. As Tracy stepped, he received another revelation, which instantly built the next column of stone to meet his footfall. As each revelation came, Tracy made a step, which made another column ascend from the deep to meet his foot. If Tracy hesitated, nothing met his progress.

The more Tracy walked, the more he understood. Soon, he saw a pathway of disconnected stones form ahead of him, with spaces of water the length of his stride between them. The columns were of stone, built of Rhema word, and were directed by Tracy into physical existence. Tracy was made to understand the gates of hell could not prevail against his walking, because it was written on the columns of stone themselves. So, from the shore, it appeared as if Tracy walked on water. In truth, Tracy was stepping out by faith on His Word.

As for Tracy the man, the experience felt like when he learned to ride a bike, and the training wheels were off. Tracy was shown how to walk on water, and he was doing it. He felt that moment of freedom, knowing he could balance and not fall. And, just like Moody was there to catch him if he fell, Tracy knew he could get up again, and walk on water again without failing. Then, Tracy heard joyous hollering and clapping. Tracy looked behind him, and it was the Lord who was in the distance cheering him on.

Tracy was astonished, but knew he had succeeded. Tracy had learned how to walk on everything Jesus and the Holy Ghost showed him, and he was well on his way.

"Aren't You coming with me?" Tracy yelled down the river.

"My Grace is sufficient," Jesus yelled back.

Tracy was incredibly grateful, although that felt woefully inadequate. Tracy wanted to thank Him, but knew that thanking Jesus was only doing what He said to do. So, Tracy kept walking, for without faith it was impossible to please Him, but that still didn't seem enough...

"Just tell everybody how to do it," the Lord answered. "They all need to start walking on water!" and with that, Tracy woke up.

Selah.

Chapter 33

- Momma Ro

After Tracy learned his family's bloodline, his assignment was complete. The next day a recruiter called. Tracy traveled to Dayton for an interview the following day, and the next day he went to work there. By the end of the week, they asked Tracy to work from home while they got a contract ready for a project. The following week, Tracy was handed a company credit card, and, within two weeks of learning the family bloodline, Tracy was off to Washington, D.C. with a job, traveling expenses, and a new direction in life.

As Tracy drove from Columbus, decades of memories filtered through his mind. Although D.C. wasn't Tracy's first choice for his next move. It reminded Tracy of the time when He told him to put his waterbed together. Like then, Tracy knew God was up to something, and welcomed the opportunity. At the same time, Tracy dreaded what was likely to be involved. In the back of his mind, Tracy thought returning to D.C. meant reconciling with Bobby. He hadn't seen Bobby since Freddie died eleven years earlier. The time before that was at Vera's funeral two years before that. Now that they were gone, Tracy didn't want to revisit his childhood memories of D.C.

On the other hand, Tracy didn't want to return to Columbus after his two-week contract was finished either.

"Lord," Tracy said. "I'm grateful for the progress, and I recognize what You are doing behind the scenes. But if this is what I'm supposed to do, You have to help me."

Tracy waited for an answer. None came, but that wasn't unusual. Tracy knew He wasn't under any obligation to respond to his crazy thought patterns.

"But, Your thoughts are higher than my thoughts," Tracy added.

Little did Tracy know, God had him on a fast-track. As Tracy neared D.C. he realized he would be there for dinner, so he called Todd. Over the years, the college roomies caught up with one another every month or so. Todd's diligent study habits transferred into promotions and career advancements, and Todd now lived in a wealthy suburb in a house worthy of manse status.

"Hey Todd," Tracy said. "What are you doing for dinner tonight?"

"Nothing," Todd said. "Why?"

"It happened so fast I haven't had a chance to tell you," Tracy said. "But I'm on my way to D.C. for a two-week contract."

"How wonderful," Todd said. "Once you get settled in your hotel come over. I can't wait to show you the house. Then we can go somewhere for dinner."

After he checked in to his hotel, Tracy changed his clothes to match his red sneakers. Then he drove through the planned curves of Todd's neighborhood of three thousand square foot homes. Todd answered the doorbell and gave Tracy a big hug.

"It is so good to see you," Todd said.

"You too," Tracy said, but was distracted by the height. "Your pictures didn't do the house justice," and Tracy looked down at the shined Brazilian hardwood floors, and bent to take off his chucks.

"You don't need to worry about that," Todd said.

"Yeah right," and Tracy took off his shoes.

"So," Todd said as they toured his home. "Sabrina lives down the street. I am sure she would love to come to dinner."

"That would be great," Tracy said.

"Good, because I already invited her. It's been a long time."

"It sure has," Tracy agreed, and they headed upstairs to finish the tour.

"Just after I spoke with you I called Granny," Todd said. "We hadn't caught up in a while. She told me about you living with your Dad and Mom in Columbus, and about your contract here in D.C."

Tracy listened, because Todd was obviously going somewhere in his careful way. After he showed Tracy his bedroom suite over the garage, they headed back over the catwalk to the opposite end of the second floor.

"I know this is only a two-week contract," Todd said, "but after talking with Granny," and Todd stopped to face Tracy. "There are plenty of jobs here that could use your skill set. You don't have to go back to Columbus," and Todd opened the door to the large guestroom like a game show model would gesture to see what was behind door Number 2. "So, this is your bedroom until you buy a house."

Tracy's mouth dropped open as Todd showed Tracy his room. Then, Todd's voice went away as Tracy daydreamed.

Of course Tracy was flabbergasted by the opportunity, and he knew there were many jobs in the area. If a contract ended, he could pick up another. More importantly, now he would have the security of a place to live while he saved up money to buy a house. Meanwhile, Todd went back downstairs, and he showed Tracy the details he would need to know as a housemate.

'So this is why You were so quiet Lord,' Tracy thought. 'You got all this set up while I drove here,' and then Todd stopped talking. They were standing by the alarm system at the front door.

"Tracy," Todd said curtly. "Come back to reality."

Tracy smiled, and thought it was great to be in the company of a friend who knew him so well. Todd was kind of like Freddie, Tracy thought, but it was more than that. God gives you your family, but *you* get to pick your friends.

"Tracy," Todd said again. "Do you remember the code?"

"The code?" Tracy asked, and then he saw Todd's fingers poised over the alarm keyboard. "You know I don't," Tracy admitted. "But show me again, and I promise I'll stay right here."

That night, Tracy, Todd and Sabrina had dinner together. The last time the friends gathered was after Todd's college graduation. In that tradition, Tracy did a dramatic re-enactment.

"Ok," Tracy said, and got up from the table. "I have to go to the bathroom. But before I go, there is a topic I would like you to discuss. You're both gay. Now talk amongst yourselves."

"How did we not know each other was gay?" Todd giggled.

"And now I sell pharmaceuticals to gay boys," Sabrina laughed. "I guess we have come a long way."

But that wasn't the only reunion in store. The next night, Tracy called another lifelong friend - the one he met in first grade.

"What are you doing?" Tracy asked.

"Child, the Lord must have put me on your heart," Tori answered.

"Why do you say that?" Tracy asked.

"Well," Tori said, "I have all my friends here supporting me except one, an' now you called."

"What happened?" Tracy asked. "Is it serious?"

"Not that serious," Tori said. "I just wanted to be a little thinner, an' everything is fine. I just have to be careful what I eat for a while."

"Well," Tracy said. "Guess where I am?"

Tracy told her, and Tori was beside herself. They had kept in contact over the years, but hadn't seen each other. So the first grade classmates reunited while going to restaurants to try new foods. On Wednesday they went to church together, where Tori spent all of her free time. Tori didn't tell her mother Tracy was in town, or Bunky, so the two planned their attack. After church, they headed to Momma Ro's house for Sunday dinner. Tori went to the front door and started banging.

"Bunky," Tori cried. "Come open this door!"

"Girl," Bunky yelled as he came through the living room. "What are you doin' bangin' on *this* door? You know we always come in on the side."

By the depth of his voice, Tracy realized he hadn't seen Bunky since he was a teenager.

"Quit your stallin' an' let me in," Tori yelled.

"Didn't your Momma raise you right?" Bunky chided. "Actin' like a hoodlum in this neighborhood," and he opened the door.

Tori stood broad chested with her hands on her hips to hide Tracy, but Bunky's voice belied his adult body. As Tracy peaked through Tori's elbows, he marveled at the towering six-foot, seven-inch man, who was easily two-hundred-and-fifty pounds of muscle. Before Bunky could figure it out, Tori slid to the side and Tracy stood up. Bunky looked as if he had seen a ghost, and then he picked Tracy up and tossed him around like a rag doll. He carried Tracy into the living room before he let go, and Momma Ro came out of her kitchen.

"What in the world?" Momma Ro crooned. But her tall self couldn't believe it, and the room couldn't hold her joy. Eventually, everyone settled down and Charlie came over.

"Good to see ya," he said, and grabbed a soda from the fridge.

Then they ate - fried chicken, green beans, collards, macaroni and cheese, cornbread, and a big sheet cake. Nothing had changed in Momma Ro's rancher except Tracy's size, which made the house seem small. After dinner, they went to the finished basement that brought back happy memories.

"Child," Momma Ro sang. "I've been prayin' for ya. But shoo, it's good to lay eyes on ya," and she hummed a little. "Last time I spoke to Granny, she was sayin' you were out at your father's in Ohio. I bet it was good for you to get to know one another."

"It was good Momma Ro," Tracy said, "an' it's truly great to be back here."

"Your Momma always wanted you to get to know your father," Momma Ro said. "But I didn't even know you were comin' to town sugar," and Momma Ro took a sip of her grape soda. "Have you seen Bobby yet?" and a hush fell over the room.

"Actually Momma Ro," Tracy said. "I was praying about that very thing on the way here. I know there's a reconciliation comin' between him and I. But if the Lord don't arrange it, I'm not gonna try an' birth an Ishmael. In the meantime, I'm gonna stay right where I am, an' enjoy all y'all."

"Well shug," Momma Ro said, "that sounds Biblical. Come on over here an' get yourself another piece a cake," and Tracy smiled. Momma Ro was always in the Bible, and if his answer was good enough for her, it was good enough for him, and it was great to be home.

Chapter 34

- the perfect house

Tracy's two-week contract turned into six-months, and by July he got the rest of his things from Columbus. Living with Todd was like college days, only with less drama. The D.C. market was plentiful, and Tracy got another job before his six-month contract was up. Tracy found a church home with Tori's congregation, and went to Momma Ro's every Sunday afternoon. Then, in November, the preacher at Tori's church confirmed what Tracy heard in Columbus.

"God has a perfect job for everyone," the preacher said. "Sometimes we have to find it," and the congregation cheered with 'Amens'. "And know that God has your house, the one especially picked out for you in his perfect plan," and the organ swelled. After a while, the preacher spoke of everyone's health. "And expect God to restore your body, the body Christ paid for on the cross…"

Finally, after another few minutes he said, "Oh yes, God knows your partner, sometimes even when you don't. It may even be someone you know, and had no idea was His plan. But know this: God has the perfect spouse waiting for you for the right time," and Tori squeezed Tracy's hand as a chorus of praise rang through the hall.

The preacher's words were confirmation of the four promises God gave Tracy in Pier One, although he kept that fact under his hat. As Tracy and Tori went to Momma Ro's for dinner, Tracy got an unction to swing into a new subdivision under construction.

They drove by a freshly dug pond, and then a sections of roads, sidewalks and townhouses that were built, but not finished.

"Where are we going?" Tori asked.

"I felt an impression to pull in here," Tracy said.

"Did you just hear from God?" and Tori was excited.

"Not exactly," Tracy said, "but I think we should see what's here."

"Well," Tori said flatly. "This is odd. There's nothing around here but a bunch of woods."

They stopped by the office for information. A realtor gave them pamphlets, and showed them various models and floor plans.

"I have a townhome I could show you," she offered.

"Let's take a look," Tori said.

They went to the backside of the development. The row-homes were two stories high with an untouched forest behind. The realtor went to the middle one, and Tori turned to Tracy as the realtor fooled with the lockbox.

"You always want the end unit," Tori said through her teeth. "There's more light, an' you'll only have one neighbor that shares a wall." Then, Tori said loudly, "Can we see the one on the end?"

"Well, it's not finished," the realtor said, "but you will get the idea."

The realtor went to the end house and opened the door. Tracy's first thought was that it was comfortable, because it had a lot of light. Then he looked deeper inside. There were no kitchen cabinets, countertops, carpet or flooring. The wiring wasn't finished, so there were no light fixtures, and wires spat out from boxes where sockets and switches would go.

Do you like your house? He asked.

Tracy was stunned. The realtor began her tour, but it was difficult with so much unfinished.

"How will I know what this is going to look like?" Tracy asked.

"You can go to the showroom," the realtor said. "It's not open to the public, but it's in the shopping area in the middle of…"

"Oh," Tracy said, completely sidetracked, "there's a basement?" and the realtor took them to the basement where bare bulbs hung helter-skelter in the large empty room.

"This will remain mostly unfinished," the realtor said.

"I can finish this off," Tracy decided, because he liked the open space to workout in.

"Do you like your house?" He asked again, and Tracy became intrigued.

When they went back upstairs, Tracy paid attention to the way the staircase ended at the small half-bath. The main hall also went from the front door through to the living room, and things became familiar from Tracy's vision. When he looked through the kitchen where the refrigerator would be, Tracy could see where Granny Berger had sat on the sofa that wasn't there yet. When Tori and the realtor toured the living room, Tracy went upstairs by himself.

Tracy went into the master bedroom, and recognized the shelf running above the doorframe at the odd angle. Tracy went into the master bath where there was a space for a Jacuzzi tub. It also had a double sink and a shower, both of which he always wanted.

"Do you like your house?" He asked a third time.

Tracy smiled, bit his lip and wondered. He left the master bedroom, and went down the hall to the guest bedroom. Tracy half-expected to see Freddie lying on the bed in his white sweat suit with his hands behind his head, but the room was empty. Then, Tracy understood Freddie was resting. He did what was allowed in Tracy's vision, so Freddie wasn't there in real life, yet.

"Yes," Tracy finally answered. "I do like this house. But how do I know what's ordered for it?"

"Go and check it out," He said.

"Ok," Tracy said. "I will."

Tori and Tracy went back with the realtor to her office. She asked questions in quick succession, and noted everything on her computer screen:

"Are you employed? How much money do you make? Are you a first-time buyer? What is your address? How much do you currently pay in rent?"

Papers suddenly flew out of the printer. After a few signatures Tracy thought were permission for a credit check, she was done.

"Congratulations Mr. Staples," the realtor said, and she stood to shake his hand. "You just signed a contract for a new townhouse."

"What?" Tracy asked. "What does that mean?"

"If all the numbers work out," she said, "and I didn't see any alarms, you just bought a house."

"I don't even know what it's going to look like inside," Tracy exclaimed.

"Well," the realtor said. "You can go to the showroom and see everything picked out for it."

"What if I don't like it?" Tracy asked.

"Of course, you can change things," the realtor said, "but it will cost $1,000 per change order," and she made a boo-boo kitty face. "Sorry about that."

At Momma Ro's, Tori explained in great detail how Tracy bought a townhouse basically sight-unseen. Then, Tori decided Tracy needed to plan. They went to Pier One that afternoon, where Tracy first heard about his perfect house. He always envisioned his kitchen with a copper-colored scheme. Limited edition copper charger plates were on clearance, so he bought them. The next day, Tracy told his co-workers the whole story: the vision of the townhouse, repeating the promises, buying the townhouse before it was finished, and buying his charger plates.

"You matched plates to your house before you moved in?" his co-workers asked.

"I bought them on faith," Tracy said. "The Lord told me to."

"That's really cool."

Because the realtor thought Tracy might change his mind, she made an appointment for him to see the showroom after work. Everything was exactly what Tracy wanted. There would be wall-to-wall carpeting in every bedroom and on the stairs. It had recessed lighting, a plush beige living room carpet, maple floors in the hall and dining room, gray granite countertops, cherry wood cabinets, and stainless steel appliances - all of which were masculine. Because Tracy skipped the living room on the tour, he realized God provided the fireplace and mantel he always wanted as well. When the design team finished showing the samples, Tracy giggled and thought, 'God does know the secrets of your heart', and he didn't want to change a thing.

But not everyone agreed with the plan for Tracy's new house, specifically, Tracy's project lead and the Director of Human Resources. Since his visions in Chattanooga, Tracy recognized demons and evil spirits more easily. They tried to manifest themselves in those who allowed such manipulation. They could inhabit so-called 'friends', and oftentimes family.

However, particularly in contract work, the spirit of jealousy was busy. The fact that God was no respecter of persons allowed the spirit of division to flourish, disguised as racism. This circumstance, along with jealousy, made Tracy a perfect target.

Five months earlier, Tracy had a contract that didn't make much sense. Accounting anomalies kept appearing, and Tracy couldn't fix them. After a few months, the H.R. Director called Tracy in to announce he was being put on a Performance Improvement Plan. Her name was Dixie, who was a small painted woman in a business skirt, blouse and blazer, topped with well-appointed brunette hair and blond highlights. As Tracy sat in her office, he detected a veneer about Dixie, which reminded him of the dart in the eyes of the demon he slew with the help of the annoying angel.

In speaking with other co-workers, Tracy learned the project lead's father was on the board of the company. This was also the project lead's third assignment in four months. The project lead was from Alabama, and was more racist than anyone Tracy had ever met. Tracy also figured out that the project lead planned to use him as the fall guy for his own incompetence.

The upshot was that Tracy knew the Performance Improvement Plan was bogus, and that Dixie's H.R. Department was the reason the project lead was still employed by his father's company.

Months later, and about the time Tracy was led to his townhouse, Tracy worked with a lovely woman from Canada on the project. She didn't understand racism, and wasn't familiar with American mores. They had been working together for weeks when Tracy found out the truth: the racist project lead that hired Tracy directly lied to him, and the accounting anomalies had occurred months before Tracy arrived on the scene. Tracy was furious, so that night he prayed.

"What should I do Lord?" knowing He knew everything about it.

"Let them have it," He said.

So, Tracy stayed up all night to fix a process two teams had tried to fix over the past five months. 'Swirl Sutra' kicked in, and by morning, Tracy had written five different manuals. He laid them out at work, which took two eight-foot tables to spread out the documentation - from legacy mapping, to testing and training, to go-live; all of which included screenshots for each individual step with idiot-proof arrows. When Tracy finished his presentation, the team of eight looked at him in absolute awe.

"Yeah," Tracy laughed. "You won't see me after this, because I just finished the project for you."

Then, Tracy and his co-worker from Canada presented the new accounting process to the client. They were astonished. After the meeting broke up, Tracy and his Canadian co-worker waited by the elevator.

"I think that went well," Tracy said.

"You know it did boy!" she screamed, and thoroughly grabbed Tracy's tight round black ass.

Tracy immediately looked at everyone through the glass of the boardroom, in order to confirm they saw what happened. Sexual harassment was a real and present danger in the highly politicized world of contracting in the nation's capitol. So, Tracy placed his cards of racism, and the pronounced smack on the ass by his co-worker in an imagined sealed envelope in his breast pocket. Then, Tracy got on the elevator with his Canadian colleague, and they had a great lunch together. Later, as Tracy brushed his teeth and got ready for bed, Tracy got another directive.

"If you have any work you want to keep on that laptop, get it off." He said. *"Then clean the laptop, change every password to Live Life Out Loud, and make sure you capitalize the L's."*

"What's going on Lord?" Tracy asked.

"Tomorrow they are going to terminate your contract."

"Really?" and Tracy was surprised at first, although it started to make sense as he listened to God's plan.

"But I want you to be ready for it. Dress in casual clothes, do not show up to work before ten, and make plans with Tori to have lunch at eleven."

Because the project lead and his father's company had been so openly hostile to him, Tracy took God at His word - particularly about the 'Loud' part. He put on a powder blue shirt, ivory bow tie and pants, and the woven slip-ons he bought with Harry. Looking ready for at least nine holes, Tracy went to work precisely at ten-o'clock carrying his freshly wiped laptop.

"You look snazzy today," the secretary said. "Let me see what cubical they are putting you in for the next project," and she searched her schedule.

"I don't think I'm staying," Tracy said, "but please verify that."

The secretary made a call and looked at Tramele – the name Tracy now used at work – because she was surprised.

"You're right," she said. "H.R. would like to see you now."

"Good," Tramele said. "I was counting on that," and Tracy went to the H.R. Director's office.

"Have a seat Tramele," Dixie said.

She was wearing a different version of her power skirt and blazer. Tracy took a seat in his ivory pants, put the laptop down next to his chair, and crossed his legs to accentuate his woven slip-ons.

"How did you like your last project?" she asked.

"It was ok," Tramele stated. "A little challenging, but I made it through successfully. Yet I am grateful it's over, and I am ready for the next new thing."

"Well," Dixie said, "that's exactly what we want to talk to you about. We have put a separation package together for you. We are going to terminate your contract," and Tracy wondered if she had a mouse in her pocket.

"Well good," Tramele decided. Dixie looked up. "I did hear you correctly, didn't I?"

"Excuse me?" Dixie asked, and was perplexed, but Tracy recognized the enemy.

'The Blood has already been spilled', Tracy thought. 'Here's my time to testify, and I can watch Satan be defeated in all of this. I can kick the demons of jealousy and racism's ass right in front of her heathen eyes', and Tracy smiled. 'You think you have me cornered?'

"So," Dixie said. "We have drawn up a separation letter, and we will forget all about that Performance Improvement Plan."

"Which I passed successfully," Tramele stated.

"Yes," Dixie said. "Right," and went on as if that had no bearing on the matter. Then, she produced a large business check from her folder, and laid it next to the separation letter. "We will also give you a separation check for seven thousand dollars."

Tracy knew what Granny would say: 'You can keep your damn check!' Instead, Tracy looked at her, unfolded his legs, folded his hands and leaned forward to see her eyes.

"The Lord is telling me not to sign that document because it has a string attached," Tracy stated. "And the string is that check, to ensure I can't sue your company for sexual harassment."

The H.R. Director was stymied, and the enemy was frozen.

"So," Tracy explained, "I am going to have to decline your offer and give you back your laptop, tell you the password and leave, because I have lunch plans in twenty-minutes." Then, just to mess with her, Tracy pulled back his powder blue sleeve and looked at his wrist as if a designer watch was there.

"Excuse me?" Dixie repeated.

"Again," Tracy said from his seated position. "I prayed about this last night, and God revealed to me your plans. So, if we're done here, can I go?"

Dixie looked at him, blinking.

"Do you actually think I dress this way to come to work?" Tracy added.

Then, Tracy picked up the company laptop, stood, went to the desk, and put it on top of the unsigned agreement and check. The eyes of the H.R. Director watched but she was powerless to move, just like the darting eyes of the doomed demon. Then, Tracy calmly took a post-it note and pen from her desk. He wrote: 'Live Life Out Loud', stuck it to the computer, and went and opened the office door.

"You have a great day," Tracy said without turning.

"Sorry you won't be able to get your townhouse," Dixie taunted.

"Stop Tracy," He said. *"Shut the door,"* and Tracy did as he was told. *"Turn around and say this:"*

"Excuse me?" Tracy asked, the same way she had.

"Well," Dixie said acerbically. "You have to have a job to buy a house."

"Say this Tracy:" He said, and Tracy did:

"Who says I have to have a job to get a house?" Tracy asked.

"Every mortgage requires you have employment," Dixie said lawfully.

"Move over Tracy," He said, and Tracy watched these words come from his own mouth:

"Those are Man's words. God's words were before the foundation of the world, and He says He will give me goodly houses that I did not build, wells I did not dig, and vineyards I did not plant. I am going to get this house, and, expect a phone call from me rejoicing with a follow-up testimony of just how good the Lord is!"

Then Tracy opened the door, walked out, and got to the parking lot before he asked.

"Lord, what just happened?"

"You were supposed to go to closing on the house today, and they knew it."

Now, it was Tracy who was shocked at the depth of their deviousness.

"Do not worry about it Tracy," He said. *"They are not going to be ready for closing today or tomorrow. It will be next week."*

"So what are we going to do?"

"Well," and the Lord smiled. *"We are going to start this car and have lunch with Tori, and talk about all the good things I have done."*

"Yeah," and Tracy smiled. "Let's do that."

Chapter 35

- Tracy at the Soirée

After lunch with Tori, Tracy went back to Todd's and prayed. He acknowledged what God had done, and that he was about to own a house. Tracy also wondered how he would pay for it, so he asked.

"Go back to repeating what I promised you," He answered, *"and thank Me for it every morning. Whenever you feel uneasy through the day, say it Out Loud."*

"That's gonna be a lot of prayin' Lord," Tracy said.

"It will be a lot of saying to see it," He said.

So Tracy did. He said his prayer before he searched for a job. If anxiety hit as he waited for people to call, he said it again. Tracy said it while he worked out, and during lunch. Sun up to sun down, Tracy repeated God's promises for five days. However, when Todd was around in the evenings, Tracy didn't say it aloud. Tracy knew Todd wouldn't understand until he saw God get Tracy his house. Todd was also distracted, because at the end of January he was hosting his fortieth birthday party.

After Thanksgiving, Tracy and Sabrina had stuffed translucent pearlized envelopes that announced *"La Noire Elegant,* (also known as) The Old Black Stank Soirée". The party was a multi-day event, and Todd had prepared all year. The basement's remodel included a grotto style bath. The back wall of the niche was lit for a life-sized Grecian woman who carried cement fruit, and her nude beau held towels for the shower.

There was only one thing left to install, which blocked Tracy's entrance when he came back from an interview. The large red leather couch took up the front hall, and was stuck at an absurd angle into the white leather couches of the living room. Todd stood behind it.

"Ta-da!" Todd said. "What do you think?"

"It's awesome," Tracy said, "but I'm not sure it looks good here."

"Silly," Todd said. "I had it custom made and delivered for the basement." Tracy wondered why the couch wasn't fully delivered, but Todd was undaunted.

"Come on, put your stuff down and help. Then we can go eat dinner real quick, and sit on my new couch and watch TV on my new flat screen."

But the stairs to the basement were as grand as the rest of his home in style elements only, and the couch got stuck at the first turn.

"Careful with my leather," Todd said. "I can patch a wall."

Four hours later, Tracy called a time out.

"I think somethin's wrong with this process."

"I guess you're right," Todd admitted.

"So, are you gonna send it back?"

"Hell no!" Todd exclaimed. "This bitch is going into the basement," and when Tracy came home the next day, the red leather couch was gone. Tracy followed the trail of fine white dust to the middle landing, and Todd stuck his powdered face through the couch-sized hole.

"She's in here," Todd said. "She looks good too!"

But there was another problem, which Todd explained over dinner.

"Tracy," Todd said. "I don't mean to be rude, but you're going to have to find somewhere else to be on Thursday."

"You mean, because of your out-of-town guests?" Tracy asked.

"No. They have their hotel rooms," and Todd hesitated. "But the Closed Door Party on Thursday is my inner circle, and you don't know them."

"Do not worry Tracy," He said. *"You will be in your new house."*

"Don't worry," Tracy repeated. "I understand. I'll find a place to be."

"Thank you," Todd said.

Tracy wasn't totally convinced, but he stood in faith. Then, on the Wednesday of Todd's birthday party, the title company called. They were ready to close, and wanted Tracy to come in the next day.

"Lord," Tracy said. "I don't have a job yet."

"Have you not understood anything by now?" He asked. *"What have we been saying?"*

Tracy said it: "Thank you Father, for my perfect job, my perfect house, my perfect body, and my perfect spouse."

"Good," He said. *"It is time to see what you have been saying, and you will see it tomorrow."*

"Lord, I'm not tryin' to go there an' lie."

"Just go to the bank for the certified check, take Tori to the closing, show up on time, and shut up."

'Show up and shut up,' Tracy thought.

That was pretty clear, so Tracy called Tori. Both knew the realtors were supposed to do a forty-eight hour check on employment, but when Tracy told Tori His directive, she became his aide-de-camp.

"Now remember," Tori instructed. "All we gonna do is show up an' shut up. Just sign, an' when all this is over with we're gonna rejoice, because God got you a house without a job."

They went to the small office in a non-descript building to meet with the title agency. No questions were asked of Tracy except for the check, which he handed over and signed the receipt. Tracy was handed more papers that were explained, and he signed. Explain, sign, and repeat went on for about half-an-hour, and Tracy left the office with the key to his new townhome. Because God believes in overflow, Tracy also left with a three thousand dollar check back from the closing costs, which he knew was to buy furniture.

As soon as Tracy and Tori were back in the Jeep they screamed and rejoiced, and as they went to the townhouse it started to snow. Everything was in place - the maple floors, granite countertops and cherry cabinets. Then, Tracy noticed the knobs and looked around. He went to the front door and went upstairs. Every knob and fixture in the entire house was brushed nickel, and Tracy laughed at God's joke. He loved brushed nickel, and five was the number of Grace. When they were finished rejoicing, Tori looked at Tracy.

"What are we gonna do now?" she asked. Tracy stood in the living room in front of the fireplace and mantel he always wanted. He got pensive, turned in a circle, and looked around in thought.

"We're gonna have dinner real fast," Tracy said. "Then I'm gonna take you back home, because I have my own private praise an' worship session to do."

"Why's that?" Tori asked. "Didn't we just have one?"

"I feel like there's more to this," Tracy said, still turning slowly in the middle of the living room. "I just have to ask. So I'm gonna stay here by myself tonight."

"Well," Tori decided. "You at least need a shower curtain an' a towel, 'cause there ain't no blinds."

So they left, and had a light dinner because snow had set in. Tracy dropped Tori off, and he bought toiletries, milk, bread, peanut butter and jelly. He made a quick sandwich, and put the groceries in his virgin refrigerator. Then, he flicked the switch that turned his fireplace on and sat in the middle of the floor. He thanked the Lord, drank his milk, and ate his peanut butter and grape jelly sandwich. When he finished eating, he got up and danced for joy.

"*Stop!*" He said abruptly.

"What Lord?" Tracy said.

"You are rejoicing over the wrong thing."

"What do you mean?"

"Go outside," He said. Tracy looked through his windows, and it was snowing hard.

"Will I need a coat?"

"No," He said. *"You are not going to be out there that long."* Tracy put his shoes on, because there were a few inches of snow on the ground.

"What now Lord?" Tracy asked as he stood outside.

"Grab that stake in the ground," He said. Tracy was shown the plain wooden stake at the corner of the lot. He went and wriggled it out of the ground, and the bottom was covered with mud and ice.

"Now take it, and run back in the house," He said, and Tracy did. *"Shut the door and lock it,"* and Tracy did. *"Go into the living room by the fireplace,"* and Tracy did.

Tracy held the stake so the mud and ice were over the hearthstone, warmed himself by the fire as he waited, and the mud and ice melted.

"You are rejoicing over the wrong thing," He repeated.

"What should I be rejoicing over?" Tracy asked.

"Remember back in Atlanta? When I had you reading Psalm 91 every morning for a year, until I released you from it?" and all of His words came back to Tracy, as easily as he knew his name:

Psalm 91:
He that dwelleth in the secret place of the most High
    shall abide under the shadow of the Almighty.
2 I will say of the Lord,
    He is my refuge and my fortress: my God; in him will I trust.
3 Surely he shall deliver thee from the snare of the fowler,
    and from the noisome pestilence.
4 He shall cover thee with his feathers, and under his wings shalt thou trust:
    his truth shall be thy shield and buckler.
5 Thou shalt not be afraid for the terror by night;

nor for the arrow that flieth by day;
6 Nor for the pestilence that walketh in darkness;
nor for the destruction that wasteth at noonday.
7 A thousand shall fall at thy side, and ten thousand at thy right hand;
but it shall not come nigh thee.
8 Only with thine eyes shalt thou behold and see the reward of the wicked.
9 Because thou hast made the Lord, which is my refuge,
even the most High, thy habitation;
10 There shall no evil befall thee,
neither shall any plague come nigh thy dwelling.
11 For he shall give his angels charge over thee, to keep thee in all thy ways.
12 They shall bear thee up in their hands,
lest thou dash thy foot against a stone.
13 Thou shalt tread upon the lion and adder:
the young lion and the dragon shalt thou trample under feet.
14 Because he hath set his love upon me, therefore will I deliver him:
I will set him on high, because he hath known my name.
15 He shall call upon me, and I will answer him:
I will be with him in trouble; I will deliver him, and honour him.
16 With long life will I satisfy him, and shew him my salvation.

Tracy smiled, but still didn't completely understand.
"Well," He said. *"Welcome to the secret place."*
"What?"
"Remove the dirt from the bottom of the stake."
Tracy tapped the stake on the hearthstone carefully so not to stain his new carpet, and all the mud and ice fell off as a piece. On the end that had been in the ground was clearly marked in a contractor's black marker: Lot 91. Tracy smiled, marveled at the Lord, and spent his first night in his secret place of peace.

Selah.

The next night was Todd's Welcome Party. When Tracy signed the guest book with the feather pen, he wrote his new address for the first time, and Todd came over to give Tracy a hug.

"Thank you for understanding about last night," Todd said, and then he noticed what Tracy was doing. "What are you writing?"

"My new address," Tracy said.

Todd looked at him, because Todd was still not convinced of Tracy's connection to the Lord. Todd never understood why Tracy left N.C. State, and Todd couldn't believe Tracy could buy a house so soon, particularly without a job and nothing saved.

"Really," Tracy said. "This is the address of my new townhouse."

"How do you buy a townhouse in two days?" Todd exclaimed.

Tracy shrugged his shoulders.

"How come you didn't tell me?" Todd asked. Tracy looked around at Todd's guests.

"You were busy," Tracy said. "Happy fortieth birthday my friend. You have always been there for me, and I am so grateful."

On Saturday, over a hundred revelers swarmed the house for the Old Black Stank Soirée. At some point, Tracy and Sabrina stood and admired the new red leather couch. With all the time that had passed, the long friends shared a moment of reflection amidst the din. A large platter of hors d'oeuvres was on a stand outside the VJ booth next to them, which matched the display of fruit the Grecian nude held in the niche of the grotto.

"Tracy," Sabrina said as she ate a grape. "If you could make a million dollars, how would you do it?"

"I'd write a book," Tracy answered.

Sabrina picked up a strawberry.

"Well, what's stopping you?" and she bit her strawberry and walked off, and Tracy felt a confirmation.

After Todd's party, Tracy moved into his new house and used his three thousand dollar check to buy furniture. Once he got a phone number, Tracy called Dixie, the H.R. Director - the carefully painted one with the tight business skirt and brunette hair and blonde highlights. Tracy told her the details of his brand-new townhouse before he told her his name. Before she could hang up, Tracy told her that God loved her and something happened. Tracy's praise report affected her, and Tracy heard her softly crying on the other end of the line.

Then, Tracy settled into his house. He spent evenings in front of his fireplace, or in his Jacuzzi as he praised God, and thanked Him for the good things he had done. Tracy took refuge in the dwelling meant for him, shielded from the noisome pestilence, where no evil could befall him, and Tracy lived there - just he and the Lord.

- Sifu Mo and Tracy

Chapter 36

Tracy loved his house and thought his perfect job would follow, but it didn't. He sent out résumés, had face-to-face interviews, and February came and went. Tracy had saved enough money to last through April. By mid-March the spirit of fear tried his resolve, but Tracy kept his mind on Him. He watched Christian television, held the stake with Lot 91 written on it, and held onto his four promises, but God wasn't talking. Tracy recognized the test of his spirit, and knew the Lord wouldn't take him this far to leave. Besides, it wouldn't make sense to get his perfect house without a job only to lose it - what kind of testimony would that be?

Then, Tracy received his first mortgage bill that was wrong. The amount was twice as much per month than his contract stated. He called the lending company who told him not to worry about it. They instructed Tracy to make his first payment, and said they would straighten it out later. After Tracy got off the phone, His interruption was abrupt as it was surprising.

"Do not pay the mortgage until they get the payment amount correct," He said. *"Otherwise you will affirm their error, and they will hold you to it."*

"Thank you for that confirmation Lord," Tracy said, a little miffed it was the mortgage company that got His attention. "Now, what about a job to pay for all these bills?"

There was no answer, and Tracy knew he was back on radio silence. Another week went by, and Tracy's frustration grew. He sat in his perfect house alone without the three other promised goods, and his 'secret place' began to feel like a desert.

"Lord," Tracy said. "This is really weird. So, if you are a friend that sticks closer than a brother, I'm gonna start treatin' you like one."

For the next two days, Tracy argued and fussed at the Lord. When that didn't work, Tracy went 'Granny Moody on God.'

"How dare you," Tracy yelled, "put me in this situation and not talk me through it." His words rang off the empty living room walls. "You're my father. When I call You, You're supposed to answer!"

Tracy went from rage to weeping. He beat the floor in front of his fireplace one minute, and was 'snottin' an' cryin' the next. He thought he had passed all his tests. Tracy was tired and at the end of yet another rope, but the end of this one was too close to everything he was promised. Tracy spent all night in his empty house 'carryin' on.' Finally, in the silence before morning, he stopped to catch his breath.

"Are you done?" the Lord asked.

"Yeah," Tracy said, and wiped his eyes.

"You know it does not take all that. I am always here."

"Then why weren't you saying anything?"

"Because you were doing so well. You were doing fine, and you were not sinking," which made Tracy remember walking on the water in his vision at the river. *"This is how I strengthen your faith for the next round, because we are going higher than this townhouse Tracy."*

"Ok," Tracy said, and was intrigued. "What shall we do?"

"You spent the last few months working for Me," He said. *"Now, it is time for you to take a vacation."*

"What?"

"Call Mo in Florida. You have wanted to workout, and wanted to get back to your Kung Fu for a while. You have lain that on the altar long enough. Now, I am going to give it back to you in a straight way."

Tracy was speechless because this made the least amount of sense, so the Lord clarified.

"Call Mo in Florida. Take a vacation there, and workout with him for your birthday weekend in April."

"Lord," Tracy protested. "My entertainment budget for April is $500, which doesn't include a plane ticket, or expenses while I'm in Florida."

The Lord waited.

"Ok," Tracy said flippantly. "You're gonna have to help me understand this one. Show me in the Bible where somebody needed something really bad, and You told them to go on vacation."

"Fine," He said. *"Remember Peter?"*

"Yeah," but Tracy didn't follow.

"When he needed money to pay his taxes?"

"Yeah…"

"I told him to go on vacation and go fishing," and as He said it, Tracy saw it, which was the revelation:

Even though Peter's profession was a fisherman, fishing was also his hobby. So, when the Lord told Peter to go fishing, Peter didn't take out his boat with his nets and crew. Instead, Tracy was shone Peter on vacation. He had on a straw hat, and sat on the bank of the river behind Granny's house fishing for catfish.

"Can you see it?" He asked.

"Yes Lord," Tracy said. "I see it."

As Tracy looked into the vision, he stood in the middle of the river on a stepping-stone that came from the deep to meet his foot. As before, when Tracy took another step toward the revelation, Tracy was reassured the gates of hell could not prevail against the next pillar.

"Now that you can see it," He said. *"Look closer."*

Tracy took another step. As he did, another stone came up to meet his footfall. Then, Tracy saw Peter the way he was – relaxed, as he lazily cast his line into the river.

"Do you see? Peter did not put a bait on the hook because I did not tell him to."

Tracy saw the hook was bare when it went in the water, and Tracy looked at the Lord, who now stood beside him.

"With the first fish Peter caught there was a gold coin enough to pay his taxes, My taxes, and plenty left over for Peter as a reward for obeying the first thing I told him to do: Go on vacation."

As He spoke, Tracy understood. By that time in their relationship, Peter knew the Lord well enough to only do what He had told him. Peter took one step at a time, faith upon faith, without adding or subtracting anything.

"Exactly," the Lord said. Then, He looked at Tracy with great intensity and said, *"What are you going to do?"* and Tracy smiled.

"I'm gonna call Mo an' go on vacation," and Tracy sighed, because it was finally time to reconnect.

Tracy thought of Mo's round face and high top fade, and realized they hadn't seen each other since college days. Then, even though it was just dawn, Tracy decided to call. Mo worked out early and besides, Tracy thought, the Lord told him it was ok.

"Hey buddy," Tracy said. Mo knew exactly who it was and laughed.

"Wow it's good to hear your voice," Mo said. "How long has it been?" and Tracy laughed.

The last time Tracy called Mo was right before he left Atlanta, and Tracy left behind what he thought was his dream house. Now, two Aprils later, Tracy sat in his perfect house, and was following God's instructions to go on vacation for his birthday. So, the 'power pellet' from 2003 worked. Tracy was sustained until the realization of owning his townhouse by 2005, and unknowingly, Mo was about to help Tracy manifest two more promises.

For now, Tracy told Mo the whole story – from getting his house without a job, to Peter fishing by Granny's riverbank. Mo laughed, but not as a scoff. To the contrary, Mo looked forward to what was to happen, because he was familiar with Tracy's relationship with God.

Mo was originally from New York, although you couldn't tell from how little he said. He was innately easy-going, which hid his understated, surgically precise humor. He was an average-sized black man whose stature belied his physical power. Mo also observed and remembered everything. Now, he lived outside of Fort Lauderdale, was married, and had two boys who were three and five. He had his master's degree in computer science and a good job. Mo was excited Tracy was finally coming for a visit, and when Tracy hung up, he booked his plane tickets.

Then Tracy called Tori. They hadn't spoken much the last few months, other than seeing each other in church on Sundays. When Tori asked for news, Tracy answered like the Shunammite woman answered, 'It is well,' when her only son was dead, and she went to fetch Elisha:

"Are ya likin' your new house?" Tori would ask.

Tracy would reply, "It's all good."

"Did all your blinds fit?"

"Good enough."

"How's the job search goin'?"

"It's goin'," and Tori was kept away from the period of testing Tracy went through.

So, Tori was surprised when Tracy called to say he was going on vacation. The next day, they shopped for workout clothes Tracy needed for his trip. Tracy caught Tori up on what the Lord was really up to, and at the end of the week, Tracy left for Florida.

When Mo picked Tracy up from the airport, it was as if the decades hadn't happened, except for their closely shaved baldheads. After they caught up, the discussion quickly regressed to the guttural pops and grunts that ensued when one spoke of Kung Fu. They both loved it - all of it – the discipline, diet, body awareness and philosophy. When they arrived at Mo's house, Tracy got settled into the guestroom. Then Mo had to go back to work.

"I have a few things to wrap up in the office," Mo said. "Why don't we swing by, and I can show you where I work."

"You can take strangers into work?" Tracy asked.

Mo chuckled in his little boy way. "I'm the boss," he said. "They work for me."

"I guess it has been a long time," and suddenly, Tracy's cell phone rang. "Sorry, I thought I turned this off," and Tracy didn't recognize the number.

"Aren't you going to answer your phone?" Mo asked.

"Nah, they'll leave a message," Tracy decided. "Right now I'm here with you, doing what God told me to do."

"Suppose this is your first fish?"

Tracy went blank as the two worlds collided.

"Remember?" Mo asked. "You didn't even have a chance to put bait on your hook, and you just started your vacation."

Tracy recognized the accuracy of Mo's words, and jumped to answer his phone. "This is Tramele, how can I help you?"

"Mr. Staples?" the man asked.

"Yes sir," Tracy answered.

"Are you still in the job market, and available for an interview?" the man asked.

"Yes sir," Tracy said, and looked at Mo and whispered, "First fish!"

Mo smiled widely, and went into the kitchen for some coconut milk.

"Do you have time to talk with me about this offer I have?" the man asked.

"Yes sir," Tracy said. "However, before we get started, I should tell you my plane just landed. I just started my vacation, so I am not in a place to write anything down."

"I understand," the man said.

"But if that's ok with you," Tracy said, "I have a little bit of time right now."

"I realize you're on vacation," the man said, "but do you have any other job offers pending?"

"No sir," Tracy said. Then the man spent a few minutes explaining to Tracy what the job entailed.

"Can you start work on April fifteenth?" the man asked.

"Yes," Tracy said.

"Well, I don't want you to be the fish that got away."

Tracy laughed aloud, but the man acted as if he didn't hear him.

"What compensation are you looking for?" he asked.

Tracy held the phone to his thigh.

"He's asking me to name my price Lord," Tracy said. "No employer has ever asked me to name my price. What should I do?"

"What do you want that gold coin to be?" He asked. *"It will be whatever you call it."*

At the time, the highest salary Tracy experienced was $85,000.

"Ninety-eight thousand," Tracy said, because it was just shy of six figures.

"Done," the man said.

"Really?" Tracy said before he could think. "All of that happened in ten minutes?" and at first, Tracy thought he was talking to the Lord.

"Really," the man answered. "I like your personality. If the rest of the team I am putting together have the same, we will have a great time on this project."

Tracy needed more time to process what happened, and the man knew it.

"So," the man said. "Enjoy your vacation, and I'll be in touch with you when you get back."

"Thank you," Tracy said and hung up.

Mo reappeared from the kitchen. "And?" he asked.

"You were right. That was the fish with the gold coin in its mouth."

"How much was the gold coin?"

"Ninety-eight."

Mo was impressed. "And in less than an hour."

"What?"

"You've been on 'vacation' for less than an hour, and you got your job."

"Yeah," Tracy said. "I guess I did," and the weight was lifted so Tracy could enjoy his vacation.

On Saturday morning, they went to Mo's studio lined with mirrors. He taught an adult class in the morning, and a kid's class in the afternoon. Immediately, Tracy was back in his element, and just like the old days, he didn't want to stop. That night, Mo and Tracy ordered Chinese food, watched Kung Fu movies and carried on with horrible 'Kung Fu' accents. They had to stop the action at almost every turn to catch more lightning-fast techniques. On Sunday morning, they went back to Mo's studio alone.

"Trace," Mo said, "do you have any questions for me?"

Tracy was surprised because Mo was so advanced. His previous teachers would never have offered this question. Tracy had been taught by trial and error before he was corrected, so this approach was new to him.

"Yeah," Tracy answered, "but I'm a little hesitant to ask them."

"How about I start," Mo said easily.

Tracy sat cross-legged on the floor, and for the next two hours Mo gave him an overview of the Hung Ga system, from the first form to the last. Tracy had yearned to learn this system his whole life, and it was beautiful and moving his old friend was the one who showed him. During the demonstration Mo hid nothing, and for Tracy it was like reading an open book. When Mo finished, Tracy was humbled.

"Would you take me on as a student?" Tracy asked.

"I already have," Mo answered, and with that, Tracy's path was straightened.

On the plane ride home, Tracy's past, present, and future collided. As he felt the soreness of his muscles, Tracy thought back to how his training started, when Granny decided he needed a hobby.

"Somethin' you're good at," Granny had said, "an' you can do into your old age. I got my bowlin'."

Now, Tracy smiled because God had returned him to Kung Fu. He provided the perfect teacher to guide him, and for the first time in a long time, Tracy was sore but content. Tracy felt he could finally breathe as he returned to his own house and started his new job. Then Tracy laughed, and remembered his four promises. Somehow, without him knowing it, God had pulled everything together: he got a job on vacation, he was in his new house, and he was working his body in the way that he loved. So, even though there was one left to realize, Tracy delighted in God's ways.

Chapter 37

- Freddie in Bobby's chair

When Tracy returned from his vacation in Florida, he finished the preliminaries for his security clearance. Then, he began his career as a consultant for the FAA through an independent consulting firm. Unlike many of the previous jobs that catapulted him to this level, Tracy loved every minute. He enjoyed the encouraging environment, and the fact his coworkers appreciated his knowledge and experience.

At the end of the month Tracy was paid, which caught him up on his mortgage, utilities, and filled his cabinets and fridge with money to spare. To celebrate, Tracy hopped in his Jeep and headed to Pier One. There, he got plates to match the chargers he bought months before. As he went through the aisles, Tracy remembered when he first heard the four promises in Columbus. He remembered carefully replacing the biscotti candle, before he yelled at God as Lynn looked on. Now, he was grateful for how much God had blessed him.

"What about that car you always wanted?" He asked.

"Lord," Tracy said. "I just got my first mortgage, started a new job where I actually know what I'm doing, and have finally caught up on my bills. I'm happy where I am, and I'm not looking to add another payment."

"But what about that car you always wanted," He repeated. *"Was it some kind of Australian thing?"*

Tracy smiled as the Lord dug into his imagination, and knew exactly what Tracy forgot he wanted.

"It wasn't an 'Australian thing' Lord," Tracy answered like a little kid being teased. "I thought about a Subaru when I was in Australia, because it was called an Outback. I liked it because it had all-wheel drive, and it would be a good, all-around utilitarian vehicle."

"Yes, and what do you want on it?"

"Well, I travel a lot in the wintertime to see Granny. I know the Outbacks have a winter package. While the Jeep is nice, electric windows and a sound system with a CD player would be cool."

"Yes, and what else?"

"Lord," Tracy protested. "I'm content where I am, and I'm trying to get out of debt, not add more."

"But I want to fulfill the desires of your heart, so I am searching it to see what else I can do for you."

"But Lord," and Tracy was silenced, because He was adamant.

"Move your butt out of the way so that I can bless you."

Tracy understood the 'butt' was the 'but' of his words, because what He had for Tracy was greater than he could imagine. All Tracy had to do was receive what the Lord had for him, and He confirmed this.

"Do not tie my hands, now that we are on a roll."

"Ok Lord, I remove the but," and instantly, Tracy's cell phone rang.

Tracy recognized the number. It was the recruiter he worked with through the spring to find a job. Tracy was grateful for his diligent work, so he pulled over to catch the call on the second ring.

Tracy parked Bruce in the well-lit parking lot, and he thanked the recruiter. Then Tracy told him he had gotten a job and wanted his name removed. But Tracy told the recruiter he would definitely use him when he looked for his next gig.

"And let that job go to someone else more suitable," Tracy prayed, "in Jesus' name."

Tracy ended the call, put Bruce's clutch in reverse, and looked behind to back up.

"Stop," He said. *"Park the car again and look up."*

Tracy did as he was told. He thought something was wrong until he looked up and saw the huge illuminated Subaru sign, and the fact that he was parked in front of the showroom window.

"Lord, you've got serious jokes."

"Tell me what you want," He said.

Feeling had, Tracy thought he would make this game hard for God.

"Ok," Tracy decided. "I want everything my Dad would have, but in my style. That means it would be white, have heated leather seats, a CD changer, a sunroof, but not an automatic," which Tracy was sure an Outback couldn't possibly have at the same time.

"So, I want a stick-shift with all those bells and whistles," Tracy decided.

"Can I help you?" a salesman said through the Jeep window. Tracy was startled, but opened his door and got out of Bruce.

"I think I'm looking for a Subaru Outback," Tracy said.

"We have many Outbacks," the salesman said.

Tracy looked around. "None of these speak to me."

"We have more in the back," the salesman said. "What are you looking for?"

"A white one," Tracy said.

"Ok. I believe we have five in," the salesman said.

As they headed to the back lot, Tracy recognized five was the number of Grace. When they got there, Tracy saw the white

Outbacks scattered among the other colors. Even though Tracy knew where his car was, he thought it would be fun to look at the others along the way. Like the 'Hot/Cold' children's game, Tracy knew the path, but decided to take his time. The first three white Outbacks didn't have sunroofs, and as Tracy passed them he waved his hand at them.

"Nope. Nope. Nope." Tracy said, and the salesman looked at Tracy more closely.

'Over here!' Tracy's car said eagerly. Tracy stopped in his tracks and turned to the salesman.

"Did I just hear that?" Tracy asked.

The salesman cocked his head and spoke slowly. "I'm not sure…"

Then they went to the fourth white Outback that had a sunroof, but the seats were cloth.

"This is fine Lord," Tracy said aloud, "but not what my father would drive," and Tracy thought of his father's advice - 'That material will cut you son,' and Tracy laughed aloud.

'Don't make me wait!' Tracy's car pleaded from the back of the lot.

"You have got to be kidding me," Tracy said.

Now the salesman truly wondered with whom Tracy was speaking, and Tracy answered the salesman by looking him directly in the eye.

"Well, God saves the best for last," and they went to the last row. There, Tracy's car sparkled like the final reveal in a showcase showdown.

"Surely Lord, you are joking!" Tracy said, and he walked around the outside. He noticed the moon-roof and stick shift, and turned to the salesman. "I want to test drive it."

"I'll get the keys," and the salesman ran back to the showroom.

Tracy opened the door and sat in the beige leather seat. It had the winter package with heated seats and mirrors, a rear-window defroster, CD changer, electric windows and locks. It also had wood-grain trim like Harry's Cadillac. So, Tracy thought it was neat and tidy like his Dad, but durable and sporty like himself.

"That car is not supposed to be unlocked," the salesman yelled louder than he realized. "How did you get in the car?"

"It was unlocked," Tracy said, and the salesman handed him the keys.

"Well, it can't be," the salesman said. Then he tried the doors to the surrounding cars that were locked. In a panic, the salesman went to the other side of Tracy's car, and he tried more locked doors to be sure. Tracy rolled the passenger's side window down.

"Would you like to come with me on this test drive?" Tracy asked.

The salesman was completely flummoxed, and looked at Tracy much more closely as he got in the passenger's seat.

Tracy loved his new car, and he realized what it meant to have 'God do exceedingly abundantly above all that we ask or think'. Then, without trading in Bruce and with only five hundred dollars down, Tracy drove his white Subaru Outback home that night. On Friday, he headed to West Virginia to visit Granny for Mother's Day in his new Subaru.

Then, Tracy returned to his townhouse and spent the summer settling in. As September came Tracy was given his next directive, which wasn't as pleasant. He was on his way home, although he was stopping by Momma Ro's to have dinner.

"Hey Tracy,' He said. *'It is time.'*

Tracy let out an audible groan. "Really Lord?"

"Yes Tracy," He confirmed, *"Now is the time,"* and Tracy sighed heavily, and took time to meditate on what had to happen before he responded.

"Ok," Tracy said. "I knew this was coming, I just didn't look forward to it. Now, if You confirm it and set it up, then I won't have a problem doing it. All I ask is that You go before me and make it plain, and that whatever is done in the dark, let it be brought to the light."

"*I will,*" He said.

When Tracy arrived at Momma Ro's, he found out Bunky and Tori were coming for dinner. As the family ate, Momma Ro confirmed what Tracy was told.

"Tracy," she said. "Do ya think it's time to reach out to Bobby? 'Cause he was askin' about ya at the breakfast on Sunday."

Momma Ro spoke for Charlie, even though he sat and ate at the other end of the table. He actually had the conversation with Bobby. All of the husbands who didn't go to church with their wives met at the same restaurant for breakfast. They arrived just before the first service got out. That way, the food was fresh and hot, and they got a good seat at the window. Then, they had two hours for 'man-gossip' until the second service got out, and they had to beat it back home before their wives got there.

"Momma Ro," Tracy said, and he sat back. "That is confirmation, so I am ready."

"That's great sugar," Ro said. "He says he has some pictures he wants to give ya. He thought it best to give them back directly, an' I thought so too."

"Besides," Tracy agreed. "We're approaching the anniversary of Freddie's death, an' I know he thinks about that. We're also coming up on Yom Kippur, an' we just finished celebrating Rosh Hashana."

"*Tracy,*" He interrupted, "*look at everyone's faces. They have no idea what you are talking about. Feed them slowly.*"

'I do sound crazy, don't I Lord,' and Tracy smiled before he spoke aloud.

"Hey guys," Tracy said. "The same voice I heard an' followed, that got me back here to Maryland, an' surprised everyone with getting' me the townhouse an' the new car, He spoke to me on the way here from work. He told me it was time to meet with Bobby, an' Momma Ro, you just confirmed it. I also realized the timing not only coincides with Freddie's passing, it lines up with the Jewish Holy Days of the New Year and Yom Kippur, which is the Day of Atonement."

Charlie, Momma Ro, Bunky and Tori stared at Tracy, because it made such perfect sense.

"So yes," Tracy said. "I am ready, just say when," and the silence held for a moment.

"You ain't gonna breakout them knives, or any nunchucks are ya?" Bunky asked.

"Bunky!" Momma Ro scolded. "You just stop it!"

"No," Tracy said easily. "This is not that. I won't have to spring any Kung Fu moves on him."

"Mercy!" Momma Ro cried. "I should hope it doesn't come to that," and she hummed a hard "Mmm-hmm," for emphasis.

"But since you're ready," Momma Ro concluded, "Bobby said ya should come over to his house anytime after work. He doesn't go anywhere, but he asked ya give him a call before ya come."

"You won't recognize him," Bunky said. "I was in the store a while ago, an' I heard a familiar voice call me. When I turned around, there was this frail man standin' in front of me. I didn't know who it was."

"An' you'll feel pity for him," Tori said.

After dinner, Tracy checked in with his father.

"I don't think that is a good idea son," Harry said. "I wouldn't advise it."

"Well, Momma Ro has all but set it up," Tracy said. "I can just stop by his house on my way home."

"You're going to his house?" Lynn sputtered from the other line. "Why can't you meet in public? Because you can forgive that man from a distance. You don't have to see him at home. That's just ridiculous."

"Mom," Tracy said calmly. "It will be fine, an' believe me Dad, this wasn't my idea."

"Well son, I understand He is telling you to do this, and He has prepared you," so Harry relented. "I guess we should see where this leads. But call me before this happens, so we can pray over it."

"I will Dad," Tracy said, and he did.

Midweek was close to the time Freddie died, so Tracy called his father. They prayed a prayer of protection, and that anything done in the dark would be brought to the light. The next day, Tracy called Bobby when he was about to leave work. He also stopped by Momma Ro's on the way, so she would know where he was. It had been seventeen years since Tracy had left his mother's split-level house, when he had milk tea with Granny and Vera, and they laughed at Helen Keller jokes.

Now, Tracy parked on the street. He walked up the driveway to see the man who may have willfully, or inadvertently let his mother die. The lawn was mowed, but there was tall grass in broken cracks of the driveway. Numerous oil stains on the cement hadn't been washed, which was unusual for the mechanic who had kept his cab and cars immaculate. On the walk from the driveway to the front door, Tracy noticed a box of Christmas lights stranded in the unkempt bushes in front of the house. The railing along the front steps was rusty. Cracked caulking squeezed from the window seams, and the aluminum trim was loose with moss growing on it. When Tracy pressed the doorbell, it didn't work. He knocked, and Bobby opened the door a little too soon.

"Glad you made it," Bobby said. "I wasn't sure you'd remember where the house was."

Tracy was immediately put off. Of course he knew where his Mom's house was, but Bobby looked tiny and withdrawn. He didn't look the sailor who navigated the world's seas in the Navy, had more cars than he could drive in a workweek, or captained his yacht on the Potomac to great bravado. However, Bunky and Tori's words hadn't prepared Tracy for what he saw – a scared, sleepless, timid man, who's personal lack of maintenance matched his house.

Inside the house it was dark, even though it was late afternoon. The carpet rolled with age, and looked not to have been vacuumed for seventeen years. Tracy's wingtip shoes stuck to it as he walked, and the living room was still setup for the Christmas party Vera hosted before she passed. The space where the Christmas tree stood was vacant in front of the picture window. The table that was usually there was still pushed into the corner. The spider plant Vera had kept in the big green pot was long gone.

Instead, the holiday candleholders and Christmas candy dish stood next to the empty pot, as if to guard the silence. Then, instinctively, Tracy went to the kitchen. The decorative fork and spoon with his Mom's fruit garland were overgrown with hamburger grease and dust, and the air was a far cry from the smell of cinnamon toast and milk tea.

"I got some pictures for ya," Bobby said. "I was goin' through the photo albums downstairs."

Tracy turned back to Bobby. He stood in the gloom of the living room, and Tracy was again taken by how small he was.

"Yeah, Momma Ro told me," Tracy said, "but before we get to all that, how have you been?"

"I've been tryin' to hang in there," Bobby said. "I haven't had a good night's sleep…" and Bobby stopped, and it was as if Tracy wasn't standing in front of him.

"Since when?" Tracy asked. Bobby looked at him.

"Since Bootsie died."

"Well Bobby, that's not good. Nobody should greave that long," and they headed downstairs to the family room Bobby had finished off for Vera.

It was incredibly dark as they descended. Bobby flipped a switch, and two lights came on by the TV. It was the same set with rabbit ears that Tracy and Freddie watched when they were in elementary school. The same brown knitted oval rug they played on as kids lay before it. Bobby took a seat in his orange cloth recliner, which looked like Archie Bunker's. By its vintage the chair could have watched a current episode, except now, it was held together with patches of duct tape. Tracy sat on the couch, but kept forward for fear of what might happen to his suit if he leaned back.

"Yeah," Bobby said. "I keep gettin' woke up at one-o'clock in the morning by these loud noises outside. It's like an army goin' down the street, an' there are helicopter searchlights all around the house."

"It always happens at one-o'clock?" Tracy asked.

"And at three," Bobby said, and Tracy thought this was odd. Those were the times his Mom woke up the morning she died, when she asked for more water, and Bobby and Freddie went back to sleep. Tracy got the sense that Bobby was chased by those demons.

"What do you do about that?" Tracy asked.

"I used to go into the corner an' pull the mattress over me, but I got past that."

"You should probably talk to someone about that," Tracy said, "because you should get your sleep."

"Yeah. I got a prescription I got to pick up at the pharmacy. But I don't have any money, so I have to wait until my check clears."

"When is that?"

"The end of the month."

"That's two weeks away. How much is your prescription?"

"Ten dollars. Why, are ya gonna pay for it?"

"I believe the Lord will allow me to do that," Tracy said.

"Oh, the Lord," Bobby said. "That's right. I heard about you and," but Bobby couldn't think of how to say it, "the church. I heard that you an' Tori go to church all the time with Rosetta," and Bobby turned into his old self a little. "If anybody could turn ya around, Tori could," and Bobby looked at Tracy the way he did before he made the boys take their bikes back to Moody's truck. "Although she might be too much woman for ya."

"Bobby," Tracy stated, who was so much greater than the little boy Bobby had known. "Tori and I are just friends," and Bobby became timid again. "Now, how about those pictures."

"Oh yeah," Bobby said. "Here they are," and he reached into the side pocket of his recliner.

Bobby pulled out an envelope, and sat up to hand it to Tracy. Then, Bobby sat back and pulled a steak knife out from under his chair. He placed it on the side table next to an open can of cashews. Tracy wondered if Bobby used the knife to open the can, but it was already open, and had a pull-tab. Then, Tracy opened the envelope and thought they would reminisce, but there were only eight pictures.

'I didn't come here for eight pictures, did I Lord?' Tracy thought. 'But maybe he just wants to hear the stories behind them, and have a little company.'

So they went through the pictures and talked like old friends, even though they weren't. They laughed about Freddie's antics, skipped over the bad parts, and managed to pass about fifteen minutes.

"I got some more upstairs," Bobby said. "They're in a plastic baggy if ya wanna see 'em," and they went back upstairs to the living room. "I've been meanin' to clean the house up, but I haven't had any gumption to do it. I've also been meanin' to get cable installed, but I couldn't get up on the roof."

"Bobby," Tracy said, "the cable people go on the roof when you get it installed."

"Well, I bought this dish off this guy. I knew all I had to do was point it at the sky. But I couldn't get my buddy to go up on the roof with me an' help, so I just let it go."

Tracy looked at Bobby in disbelief. Bobby sat down in the corner chair of the living room. Tracy carefully sat on the edge of the loveseat and looked at the material. The furniture was the set his Mom had wanted for so long, and had kept immaculate. Now it was covered with dirt, and yet more oil stains. When Tracy looked up,

Bobby had forgotten about the other pictures. Instead, he reached under his chair to pull out another steak knife. He placed it on the side table between them, and there wasn't even the charade of cashews to explain the behavior, so Tracy asked.

"Bobby, are you ok?"

"Yeah man," Bobby said. "Don't mind me. I just get scared here all by myself."

"Well, turn some lights on, an' get rid of those dark corners. Get yourself some nightlights you can put all over the house."

"An' who's gonna pay for all that electricity?"

By this time, Tracy was done with him. "Are you ready to go to the store? Because it's gettin' late, an' I have to go to work tomorrow."

"Yeah, Charlie was tellin' me about that nice job you got with the FAA. An' I heard you bought a brand-new townhouse not too far from here. So you're doin' good."

"The Lord is good," Tracy said, "an' he's not finished yet, so let's go get that prescription."

Bobby locked up the house. Then they walked down the driveway and got into Tracy's car.

"Man," Bobby said, and inhaled deeply. "It still has that new car smell to it."

Tracy smiled. Bobby used to get a new car every two years, and Tracy's new Subaru was all he could talk about.

"These leather seats are heated?" Bobby asked, "an' the mirrors have defrosters in 'em too?"

As they drove, Tracy realized that was why the Lord got him a new car before he had this meeting – a meeting with the man who told him he would never amount to anything. But that was all water under the bridge, and Bobby was the worse for it.

"You should come 'round sometime," Bobby said, after Tracy dropped him off.

"I don't live too far away," Tracy said. "But I'm gettin' busy with some projects."

"Well, if you can," Bobby said, and went into his dark house, and didn't turn on any lights. When Tracy got home, he called his father.

"Son," Harry said, and he was upset. "I don't want you going there anymore. It bothers me to hear that is what you went through. You are my son, not his, and you need to tell Momma Ro about this too," which Tracy did.

"He did what?" Momma Ro screamed. "He used me to set you up, an' then pulled steak knives out on ya? Oh no shug. You ain't ever goin' back over there again. We're done with that man for good!" and they were.

In February, Bobby's son David called Tracy at work.

"Hey buddy," David said. "I don't want to bother ya, but I think ya should know Bobby died. I'm gonna have to go view the body to identify it."

"I'm sorry to hear that," and Tracy thought a moment. "But you shouldn't have to do that alone."

"Oh I'll be alright," David said, "he wasn't your father."

"But I'm your brother, an' I'm going with you."

"Well," and David sighed. "We have to go to Lynchburg."

"Why do we have to go there?"

"Because that's where he died," David said.

"Oh," Tracy said, because he knew anything with Bobby was complicated, even if he was dead. "You can tell me on the way," Tracy decided, and David did.

Bobby visited his girlfriend for Valentine's Day, which was why David got the call from the hospital in Lynchburg, Virginia. So that night, Tracy, David, and his wife drove through the night in David's black SUV. They got up early at the motel in Lynchburg, and David's wife needed some caffeine before they went to the funeral home.

"I need to stay awake," she said at the coffee shop. Then she looked at Tracy. "An' you look like you need one too."

"That's probably too strong for me," Tracy said. "Caffeine really affects me. I probably shouldn't."

"Get out," David's wife said, and hit Tracy's arm hard. "You just let me," and she stepped up to the counter. "Yes, this man wants a mega super-charged latte," which Tracy finished before they reached the funeral home, and he was affected.

After David and Tracy identified the body they met Bobby's girlfriend, who was forty years Bobby's junior. Then, David, his wife, Tracy, and Bobby's girlfriend sat in front of the funeral director's desk. As the director spoke of transportation matters, he handed David a small bag with Bobby's personal effects. As the funeral director continued, David went through the bag and handed each item to his wife, one of which was a prescription bottle.

High out of his mind on caffeine and sugar, Tracy feverishly sought out the contents listed on the bottle of pills. He thought they would be blue, but these pills were pear-shaped and yellow.

'C, I,' Tracy thought as he read. 'But her thumb is in the way. What is that other letter? An L?'

Tracy screamed and turned to David. "What's he doing takin' a sex drug? He's not supposed to be takin' that. He has a heart condition!"

"Calm down Tracy," David said. "What are you talking about?"

"That's the new weekend sex drug," Tracy said rapidly in caffeine mode. "You can take it Friday night, an' be good Sunday all the way up to when you have to go to work Monday mornin'! But Bobby's not supposed to be takin' those while on heart medication, which I know for a fact he's on, because I tried to drown his nitroglycerin pills a long time ago."

David's wife stared at Tracy, but David asked. "But why would he be takin' a weekend sex drug in the first place?"

"Well," David's wife said. "It was Valentine's Day," and she shot her husband a look with a neck crook. "Which would have been nice," she said, because Bobby's death had messed up her plans.

"But that doesn't make any sense," David said.

"Oh yes it does," Tracy said, who realized there was a fourth person in the room. Then David, his wife, and Tracy simultaneously turned to look at Bobby's girlfriend, who shifted in her chair and was Valentine's Day red.

"I got to go," Tracy said, jumped up, and got back to David's car before he fell apart from laughing.

David and his wife soon joined Tracy, and they 'commensed to 'hootin' and hollerin'. Then, David opened the bottle to check the pills, but there were others wrapped in foil inside. When he unwrapped those they were blue, which made them laugh and rock the black SUV harder. Finally, David screamed the truth:

"Pops didn't die of a heart attack, he died of a hard-on!" and that was the end of Bobby.

Chapter 38

- the Moody tractor

There were two times in Tracy's life when Moody acted like the Tall Shiny Silver Figure. The first was when Tracy was in elementary school. Moody gathered Tracy and his 'runnin' cousins' together to take a picture. Right after, he grabbed Tracy by the hand, and they hopped in his newly refurbished black 1950 Chevy Bel Air. Moody spent years restoring the car, including the original red and black-striped leather interior. Granny could have put makeup on looking into the chrome, except she wasn't allowed to drive it. Moody knew she would mess up the wide whitewall tires in some parking shenanigan.

"You're comin' with me," Moody said, and closed Tracy's heavy door. Moody got in on his side and manually rolled his window down. Tracy did the same, because it was hot and there was no air conditioning. Moody kept the original column shift, but had installed the necessary update of an eight-track tape player. At first, Tracy thought he was in trouble because Moody was so serious.

"I took this picture so you would remember this day," Moody said, and pointed at the Polaroid snapshot developing between them in the wide seat. Then they drove to Dupont City and went to a strange house, where Moody got out without hesitation.

"Get out of the car boy," Moody said.

Tracy went with his grandfather who knocked on the door. When the white man opened it, Tracy realized they had business with each other.

"Here," Moody said, and handed the man an envelope. "This is the last thing I owe ya. In thirty days, I expect to see my title in my hands free and clear or I'm comin' back." Moody leaned over to speak with Tracy. "You remember this. This is the day your grandfather paid off his house, an' he 'owes no man nothin' but to love him'."

Moody stood back up, and cut a figure with the stub of his cigar under his Eroll Flynn moustache and stingy-brim hat.

"Thirty days," Moody said into the man's eyes. "Ya hear me?" and Moody looked at Tracy and warmed his tone. "Come on let's go," and they got back into Moody's faultlessly black hardtop coupe, started her up, and proudly backed out of the driveway as "Mustang Sally" played them out at a respectable volume.

The second time Moody acted like the Tall Shiny Silver Figure was also serious, even though Tracy wasn't sure why at the time. Moody had called a Jewish man to the house, and this was the second time Tracy had seen him. The first time was a year earlier, just after Tracy moved in with his grandparents. Granny and Moody wanted to adopt him. Vera wouldn't hear of it, so the attorney drew up papers for them to be Tracy's legal guardians.

The next time the attorney came to the house was after Moody came home in his wheelchair. Bonnie was a puppy, and Moody had just finished signing an official-looking document at the kitchen table. The tri-fold legal document was on rigid paper, and Moody held it up for Tracy to see. The only thing legible was "Last Will and Testament" printed in an English typeset across the top.

"Tracy," Moody said sternly. "You're not gonna know what's in this, but remember this day, the day it was signed."

Granny, Moody and the family attorney were at the table in the meridian blue kitchen, and Tracy stood in the doorway. Then, Moody looked at Tracy from his wheelchair.

"If anything happens to me, you get in touch with this man," Moody said, and he pointed the document towards the attorney. "He'll take care of everything else," and Moody meant business.

"Ok Pawpaw," Tracy said, and studied the attorney.

"You contact this man," Moody repeated.

The severity of Tracy's Pawpaw couldn't have been more clear, or the trust that Moody put in the Jewish man who sat at his table.

Now, almost three decades later, Tracy went to Rand shortly after his birthday to visit Moody for Easter. In May, Tracy visited Granny for Mother's Day. By that time, Moody was in the V.A. Hospital in Huntington because of the gangrene on his foot. By Memorial Day, Moody was moved to a nursing home in South Charleston to be closer to home. Tracy went to visit him, and like the 'meetin's' they held through the years, Moody spoke freely.

"Hey Trace," Moody said. "Can you get me some of that ginger extract? I've seen ya usin' it with your Kung Fu trainin'. I think it's supposed to be good for settlin' you're stomach. Mine's gettin' upset from all this medication."

"Sure Moody," Tracy said.

Tracy also noted Moody had gone 'old school', returning to homeopathic remedies his family had used at the farm. Then Moody sat up and got serious, like when they went to pay off the deed to the house, or the day Moody made his will.

"Look in there for my book," Moody said, and pointed to the drawer in his nightstand. "You're gonna need this, but give it to me now so I can call her."

Tracy got the black leather address book from the drawer. Moody always carried it in his pocket protector for important numbers, and the pages were only slightly spattered with the oil and grease of a mechanic's fingers. When Tracy handed Moody his glasses, Tracy noticed his teeth weren't in. Moody always wore his dentures when he was awake. This made Tracy realize Moody had been awake for some time, and Moody noticed Tracy looking at his teeth.

"Yeah," Moody said. "They don't fit anymore, since I lost a little weight in my gums," and he fumbled though his address book. "The family attorney died some time ago, an' his daughter took over."

With those words, Tracy realized the gravity of the situation. Moody found the number, and then reached for the hospital phone and dialed. When she picked up, Moody spoke so Tracy was included in the conversation.

"Yeah, this is Kindel," Moody said. "I was callin' for you to bring those papers in," and there was a pause while she spoke.

"I'm ok," Moody said. "They got me on some new medication that makes my stomach upset, but that's not what I called about. I got Tracy here with me, my grandson. You'll remember me talkin' about him, an' now, I'm talkin' to him about you. He'll know how to contact ya if somethin' happens to me, 'cause I'm givin' him your name an' number."

She spoke again, but Moody interrupted.

"No, I know you're busy, so you don't need to talk to him. But I expect you'll be hearin' from him soon," and when Moody hung up the phone Tracy was shocked.

Things became blurry in this world for Tracy. But as Moody gave Tracy his attorney's information, he was forced to make peace with the same thing Moody already had. Later, as Tracy drove home to D.C. he asked the Lord for more time. Tracy meant he wanted Moody to live longer, but the Lord granted his request in a different way.

Two weeks later Tracy was laid off from his contract job, which couldn't have been more perfect. By June, Tracy spent weeks at a time in Charleston visiting Moody. Tracy only came home to the townhouse to cash his unemployment checks. By the time the Fourth of July came around, Moody was moved to the VA Hospital in Richmond, Virginia. Moody trusted them, and his brother Dris lived in Richmond. Tracy also realized Moody had moved himself closer to the farm and the family cemetery. Then, things seemed to become blurry for Moody. On one of Tracy's visits, Moody said something odd during one of his check-ups, and it wasn't the first time.

"Hey Doc," Moody said. "Remember when black was white, and white was black?" and Moody went on like that until the exam was over. After Tracy pulled Moody's wheelchair out of the doctor's office, he took Moody back to his room and shut the door.

"Moody," Tracy said, and sat on Moody's bed to face him. "No one knows what you're talking about. Now, the medical power of attorney was just signed over to Granny an' me. So you need to tell me what this is all about, or not mention it anymore. Granny is tryin' to claim you as unfit, and I'm not about to let that happen. So tell me what you're talkin' about."

Moody got an odd, far away look. "Beware of the time when they call good bad, an' bad good," and he never mentioned it again.

By the time fall came, Tracy had a good amount of time to cope with the process. Tracy had spent a lot of time with Moody, so he went to visit Granny. It was October, and Granny loved Halloween. She spent all year 'yard salein' and collecting creepy doodads to spread around her porch and yard. For some reason, there were more witches in her collection than most. Granny also liked to put everything up early so everyone could admire her display.

Moody hated the process, but liked the decorations once they were up. However, Moody's real beef was with the Christmas lights, which Tracy thought about as he and Granny stuffed the scarecrow. It always sat to the right of the front door in an old webbed lawn chair, and was made from Moody's old work clothes. Tracy smiled as he remembered...

"Why does she have to wait for the coldest day of the year to do this?" Moody griped. "We coulda done this in October when we put up Halloween, an' just not lit 'em 'til now."

Granny spookily appeared in the front doorway with a box of Christmas lights.

"Aw hell no," Granny stated. "I'm not gonna leave lights up like they've been left up all year. Nor do I wear white after Labor Day," and she dropped off her box, and went back into her warm house.

A year or two later, when Tracy was in high school, Moody decided to get on Granny's nerves. It was a particularly cold and windy day after Thanksgiving. Tracy was on the ladder, and Moody sat in his wheelchair on the front porch handing him the lights.

"Here we go again in this damn cold," Moody muttered. But he stayed silent when Granny came out to get the mail. Tracy prepared himself, because he knew if they were both quiet when they were together, somebody was 'plottin' a scheme'. As Granny went down the walk to check the mailbox, Moody saw his opportunity.

"Hey Jackie," Moody said. "Since you're down there, can ya get me my hammer?"

Granny was halfway to the garage before Tracy asked the obvious through tight lips:

"What's that got to do with hangin' these lights?"

"Shhh," Moody hushed. "Don't say nothin'."

Granny got it, came back up the walk, and laid the hammer at the foot of Moody's chair. She turned back down the walk because Troy, the mailman, had just arrived. He liked to chat with all his clients, sometimes twice. There were only three houses past Granny's before he would come back down the other side of the street. That would only be a few minutes, depending on how long Barbara caught Troy's ear.

For now, Granny said hello, and only got a few tidbits of gossip before she walked back to the house.

"Hey Jackie," Moody said, "since you're goin' in the house, there's a screwdriver on the steps by the back door," and Granny went into the house with the mail.

"She must know somethin's up by now," Tracy said from his ladder.

Moody stayed mum. Granny came back with the screwdriver and handed it to Moody, who put it at the foot of his wheelchair with the hammer.

"Thank you," Moody said, and Tracy grimaced.

'You know you messed it up now,' Tracy thought. 'You never say thank you,' but Moody continued on his quest.

"Down in the basement, there's that pair of yellow-handled pliers," Moody said, and Granny went back down the walk, passed her mailbox, and went back down into the garage.

"Maybe she's quiet because she's feelin' the joy of the holiday season," Tracy mentioned.

"That, an' she wants her lights up," Moody mumbled.

About that time, Troy reached William Russell's house, and William Russell came out to get his mail. Granny waved and came back up the walk with the pliers, and put them by the hammer and screwdriver.

"Oh, an' ya know what?" Moody said. "I forgot to tell ya, while you're down there..."

"Aw shit Moody," and Granny straightened up. "Get up an' get it your own damn self!"

Troy and William Russell watched Granny slam the door to her warm house, delighted to witness the pair in action, and Moody and Tracy broke into snickers...

Now, twenty-five years later, Granny looked at the finished scarecrow.

"Ya know," Granny said. "Y'all always wanted to hang the Christmas lights at Halloween-time."

"I was just thinkin' about that," Tracy said. "An' the time Moody had you runnin' everywhere."

"An' I told the man in the wheelchair to get up an' get it his own damn self?"

"That was classic Granny," Tracy said and Granny smiled, but not for long.

"You wanna hang the lights up now?"

"No Granny," Tracy decided, "because I know you hate that. Besides, I plan on comin' back before Christmas. I can hang them then," and Granny nodded.

"But I was thinkin'," Tracy said. "We should all go down and see Moody - the whole family. We can all pile in our cars an' just go," and Granny agreed.

So, Tracy spent the next two weeks rounding up the family, and then he helped drive everyone down to Richmond. His other cousin Demi and her family drove up from Charlotte. Then, all the 'runnin' cousins' had a great visit with their Pawpaw over Columbus Day weekend. When they returned, Tracy spent the night in his room, and when he came in for breakfast Granny had just hung up the phone.

"That was Moody's doctor," Granny said. "He said Moody woke up this mornin' an' told the doc he felt really good. Then he asked when he could go home," and she paused. "'I'm ready to go home', was what he said."

Tracy looked at her.

"Now Tracy," Granny said. "The doctor said that in his experience, when he an' the other docs have seen this happen, they have anywhere from eight to twenty-four hours."

Immediately, Tracy stood even though he was numb. He picked up the phone and called Moody to keep his spirits up.

"Well Moody," Tracy finished, "I'll make plans to come down there tomorrow."

But the next morning, Granny got the call Moody had passed. The man who had stood next to the Tall Shiny Silver Figure when Tracy was three went to be with Him. 'Pawpaw. You. Pawpaw. You.' Tracy remembered when they stood side by side, except Moody didn't know that until now. Now, Moody was with Him in the heavens.

Back here, Tracy covered his pain with urgency. He and Granny systematically told his cousins, particularly Mia, who was a nurse. Tracy knew she had to be told in person, because she and Moody were so close. Tracy went and spoke to her supervisor first.

"Now she's going to know why I'm here," Tracy told the charge nurse. "So, as soon as I come around the corner an' she sees me, I'm gonna have to take her home. She'll be no use after that."

In terms of the funeral arrangements, they were taken care of by the veteran himself. Moody was to be buried at the farm, and Dris, Moody's remaining brother, just had to be there to open the gate. So Tracy headed to the farm in Virginia. Dris met the family at the motel by the lake, because no one had lived in the farmhouse for years. They had a big dinner at the restaurant, and as Dris and Tracy carried on the family realized how close they were. The two had also spent a lot of time together in Richmond with Moody the past few months.

The next day, everyone went to the small white church founded by the great Mr. Moody where his son lay in the casket. There was a respectable congregation, but all of it was a blur to Tracy. Granny ran around as if she hosted a tea party, but Tracy couldn't let go. After the service, the funeral directors asked everyone to leave to close the casket. Tracy stayed behind with Demi. The cousins sat in the center of the middle row as they turned the crank to lower the body. When Tracy couldn't see Moody's face anymore, he broke into a cold sweat and cried more than he ever had.

As the funeral procession made the last turn to the farm, nothing was familiar to Tracy. The watermelon field was covered with twenty-year-old Virginia pine. The tobacco-drying shed was hidden in young woods, rather than the hand-built building of logs that had stood at the end of the neatly planted field. When they pulled up to great Pawpaw's house, it seemed much smaller than Tracy remembered. Mrs. Moody's rocking chair still sat on the front porch, but her chicken house was gone. When they pulled into the circular drive, Tracy thought of her funeral. He remembered the tables of food, and the long procession that walked from the meadow after the rain stopped, before the bees resumed their work in her peach trees.

Now that it was fall, everything seemed tired and dying. The small family of twenty arrived, including the new generation of cousins. They were the same ages as Tracy and Freddie when they had first visited the farm. Then, just past the house, Tracy noticed a line of cars parked in the other end of the circular drive.

As the family got out of their cars, what seemed a small army got out of theirs. The distinguished black men wore black tuxedoes with white gloves, and a white apron with a triangular pattern embroidered in gold. Some had large necklaces with medallions, one had a top hat, and all had a golden 'pocket protector' on the outside of their breast pocket bearing the insignia of the freemasons. A tall elder of the group came over to Dris and shook his hand.

"We saw that one of our own was goin' home," he said. "We got everybody together. If we had known, we could've done a better job. We just found out from the obituary in the paper a few days ago."

"Moody was a Mason?" Tracy asked, who couldn't believe he didn't know this.

"And has been for a long time," the gentleman said. "He was one of our eldest fellows, and, if you don't mind, we'll take care of him from here."

The group of thirty formed a line to take Moody's casket to the gravesite where they performed the burial rite. And it made sense the son of brick maker who lived in Virginia close to one of the oldest black lodges in the country would be a freemason. Tracy also remembered when Moody commented when Mr. Wilson died, the one who taught him to be a mechanic. Moody saw the Mason insignia by his obituary in the paper. Moody said that he didn't know Mr. Wilson was a Mason, but that was the only clue he ever gave that he was one as well.

Now, what followed was the pageantry and precision of a perfectly executed service. It was a meaningful tribute to a man who had done so much with his life, and, as with so many things with Moody, it was more than anyone expected.

Once the Masons said their goodbyes, the family went through the house and time had taken its toll. Without the presence of Emma or Richard, what remained seemed shrunken and decayed. Much of the furniture was gone, and it was clear no one lived there. Before he left, Tracy went over to the equipment shed where the family tractor stared blankly at him. He thought of Moody's 'rabbit huntin', when he had shot out the tire. Then, it registered how easily Moody fell asleep at the farm. Now, his Pawpaw was finally laid to rest where he began, and his course was done.

After that, Tracy left Granny in Virginia to take care of paperwork. As he drove back to West Virginia his thoughts wandered. Moody was there for him so easily, Tracy thought, and they were such kindred souls. Moody always supported him unconditionally, and helped let him live his own life. Now that he was gone, Tracy was surprisingly lost, and Tracy realized how much the fact Moody was in this world had steadied his existence.

When Tracy got back to Rand, he headed to the house to spend the night in his room. However, when his hand touched the latch on the gate, he saw the scarecrow on the front porch. Because it wore Moody's clothes it was Moody's size, and the fact the scarecrow sat in a webbed lawn chair on the dark porch made things surreal.

So, Tracy took his hand off the latch, and decided to walk down the street to spend the night at his cousin Marie's house. He was exhausted, but as Tracy turned a rabbit came from the side of the house by the garage. Tracy wasn't sure if Moody was 'messin' with him', but the rabbit came right for him. Between that and Granny's witches, Tracy beat it to Marie's house, and the rabbit chased him the whole way.

- Moody, before he passed

- Tracy in his townhouse

Chapter 39

"Tracy," Granny said. "Come here an' tell me if you see this too."

Granny was at her sink. She looked at her cherry tree, which still had the rusted pulley attached to the trunk from when she terrorized Moody with the rubber snake. Tracy had just gotten up, and he came and stood next to Granny.

"He's looking right at us," Tracy conferred, and Granny was surprised.

"How you know it's a he?" Granny asked.

Tracy laughed. "Well, either it's the same rabbit Marie saw down in her yard yesterday, an' Mia saw across town on her lawn, or we've got an infestation."

"But he's just sittin' there, starin'," she said in amazement.

"I can't explain it either Granny. But it looks exactly like the one that chased me down to Marie's house when I first got back," and Tracy got some coffee. Granny had stayed an extra day at the farm, and Tracy wanted to get her settled before he had to get back to D.C.

Once Tracy got to Rand, he got a call from his recruiter. He was to start his new contract job on Monday, and Tracy recognized God's perfect timing. He had been unemployed since June, which afforded him as much time as possible to spend with Moody until he passed. As soon as that was finished, Tracy got a job before he could ask for it, and he was grateful.

However, when Tracy returned home and went back to work, he became angry with God. He knew his contract with D.C. Metro wasn't permanent - the problem was his empty house. When he returned alone, the emotional pain of Moody's passing that had built up in Tracy came unleashed. Tracy didn't see the point of going on, and thought he would rather be with Him, Moody, Freddie and his Mom.

"Lord," Tracy prayed. "I know this new contract isn't my perfect job, and I'm glad I have a job," and he sobbed, as the grief of Moody's death overpowered him. Then, Tracy exhaled quietly:

"I am tired of going through life experiences alone."

Tracy heard what he said and cried more. As Tracy waited, he sat in the middle of the hollow living room in front of the fireplace. The house was still empty, except for the end tables on either side of his burgundy couch, which matched the circular black walnut coffee table Moody made for Granny as a wedding present. Tracy sat cross-legged on the floor, and the emptiness grew in every direction until it engulfed him. The loved ones who had showed him his townhouse were gone - Granny Berger, his Mom and Freddie. Now that Moody was gone, it seemed to Tracy there was nothing left, and that he got something wrong.

"Where's my wife?" Tracy yelled, and he hit the carpeting. "If you can't produce the perfect wife that the four boxy walls of the church says I'm supposed to have, then I don't want to do this anymore! I'm still alone, I don't have the desire for a woman or a family, and I'm approaching forty. I should have been settled by now," and Tracy punctuated his words with more carpet hits, "and not be alone!"

There was silence, except for the echo off the blank white walls and tall ceiling.

"Everybody tells me to settle down," and Tracy sobbed. "Momma Ro and Tori are all about it, because they, 'know me so well.' Lynn, and even Dad… 'It's about time son,' he said," and Tracy stood up. "Time for what?" and Tracy looked upward and screamed. "I don't want to go through any more of life's experiences alone!"

Then, Tracy panted and spun in a circle, the way he did when he first praised God for his house.

"And Lord," Tracy clarified. "We already know shopping can be a life experience. Remember Pier One and the four promises? So change me. Make me desire a wife," and Tracy took a breath. "Because I can't make that up. I don't rap. I'm not LL Cool T, or even MD Cool T. I don't know how to rhyme. It's not my poem, it's Yours! But there's something not working right, so I must be doing something wrong."

"Are you ready for this?" He said like a remix DJ.

"Yes!" Tracy cried. "Bring it on!" and was so relieved to hear His voice. "I am ready for You to give me the desire for a wife!"

"Sit down," He said.

Tracy went over to the burgundy couch and prepared himself.

"Are you really ready for this?" He asked. *"For real?"* and then, in the process of sitting down, Tracy felt Him push Tracy into the couch with His presence of an overabundance of love. *"Am I the creator of everything?"*

"Yes Lord," Tracy answered. "Everything I see and don't see. You have created it all, and I am ready for You to create me anew," and Tracy thought of Adam and his rib that made woman, and that somehow God could change him so he would suddenly like girls.

"No Tracy," was the immediate answer, and He asked again, *"are you REALLY ready for this?"*

Tracy cleared his mind as best he could, so he could receive His peace.

"Am I the creator of the universe?"

"Yes Lord. You created it all."

"What about the languages, you know, like the 'words coming out of your mouth'?" and Tracy saw those exact words come out of His mouth in smoke as He spoke them. The wispy words swirled around Tracy's face, as if they came from the caterpillar's pipe.

"Yes Lord. All of that," and Tracy was impatient.

"So, what did I promise you?"

As Tracy said it, the Tall Shiny Silver Figure's robe became vaguely academic, and He had a pointer in His hand. He floated a foot or so above the living room floor, and stood in front of a chalkboard. As Tracy spoke, the words became a poem on the board, and He tapped each line as they were heard and became manifest:

"You promised me a:

　　Perfect Job,

　　Perfect House,

　　Perfect Body, and a

　　Perfect Spouse."

Tracy added "In Jesus' Name," and as he said it, he realized it: "And those were *Your* promises, because it has *Your* name on it. So where's my wife?"

He turned around quickly and spoke faster. *"I never promised you a wife Tracy, I promised you a spouse."*

"What?" Tracy asked, and instantly, Tracy felt Freddie's excited whisper in his ear:

"Chicken-butt! - Take a slice an' eat it up - two-cents-a-cup - don't try your luck - Chicken-butt! - Say what!?!"

Then, just as quickly, Freddie cackled with the satisfaction of decades, was gone before Tracy could turn around, and the Tall Shiny Silver Figure smiled.

"Freddie has been waiting to do that to you in your new house," He explained, *"ever since I allowed him to show it to you in that vision."*

"How is that even possible?" Tracy asked.

"Do you really want more pearls?" He asked.

"Yes Lord," Tracy said dogmatically. "More pearls please."

"Ok, I will give you two," He said. *"The first one is, 'Absent from the body, present with the Lord.' The other is that you should praise the Lord, because 'He inhabits the praises of His people',"* and He leaned into Tracy again. *"When I come to inhabit - meaning to live there, I do not come alone,"* and Tracy felt a wink. *"I come with a cloud of witnesses, and Freddie is amongst them thanks to you and Lynn,"* and remarkably, that explained both pearls.

"But enough of that for now," He said, and went back to His chalkboard. *"Back to this poem,"* and Tracy's four promises reappeared along with His pointer as He turned.

"Now," He stated. *"If I am the creator of the universe, and I created all the languages, and the 'words that come from your mouth'* (and the words appeared again in smoke around Tracy's head). *Do you not think I could come up with a word that rhymes with house?"*

Tracy didn't understand, because the conventions of this world were too calloused in him.

"Do you not think I could come up with a word that rhymes with house, yet means wife?" and the Tall Shiny Silver Figure pointed to the word 'spouse' on the board as He said 'wife'. Then, He turned to Tracy with great love in His heart.

"I do not have a wife for you Tracy, I have a spouse," and this time, Tracy was shown what He meant.

"Ok," Tracy said. "This goes against everything I have ever been taught in this world," and Tracy recounted the hours he spent in church. "They always told me out of *Your word* that homosexuality was an abomination. So, I don't know how to go forward with what You are tellin' me right now. I need You to order my steps Lord, and show me where this is in Your word."

"Fine," He said. *"Open your Bible to First Timothy, Chapter Four."*

Tracy reached for his Bible on the end table, and he and the Lord had Bible study.

"So, Paul is writing along," the Tall Shiny Silver Figure explained. *"When he is suddenly interrupted,"* but Tracy didn't understand. *"Read the first line."*

"Now the Spirit speaketh expressly," Tracy said, and understood who was speaking. "You're right Lord, the Holy Spirit interrupts Paul."

"I allowed the Holy Spirit to interrupt Paul at that time specifically for this day in age, and for this revelation to get out at this time."

Instantly, a giant pillar came up underneath Tracy's feet. The pillar stopped and became an ottoman, and because his feet were lifted up Tracy was forced to recline.

"And you can rest in that," He said, and Tracy understood the scripture inscribed on the pillar:

Psalm 110:1

The Lord said unto my Lord, Sit thou at my right hand, until I make thine enemies thy footstool.

Then, as Tracy looked at the pillar he understood who his enemy was, and the Lord explained the revelation He had saved for this present day:

1 Timothy 4:

4 Now the Spirit speaketh expressly, that in the latter times some shall depart from the faith, giving heed to seducing spirits, and doctrines of devils;

2 Speaking lies in hypocrisy; having their conscience seared with a hot iron;

3 Forbidding to marry, and commanding to abstain from meats, which God hath created to be received with thanksgiving of them which believe and know the truth.

4 For every creature of God is good, and nothing to be refused, if it be received with thanksgiving:

5 For it is sanctified by the word of God and prayer.

"Who is speaking?" the Tall Shiny Silver Figure asked.

"Paul was," Tracy said, "but he is interrupted. So now, it's the author of the Bible - the Spirit, not Paul who is speaking expressly."

"When is this going to happen?" the Tall Shiny Silver Figure asked.

"In the latter times," Tracy answered.

"And who is departing from the faith, and giving heed to seducing spirits, and doctrines of devils?"

Tracy found this hard to believe, but there was only one true faith spoken of in the Bible.

"Who is speaking lies and hypocrisy Tracy?" He asked.

"They do Lord?" Tracy asked.

"Yes. They mean well, but their conscious has been seared."

"I don't understand," so He showed Tracy as He said it:

"You see them at every Pride gathering," and Tracy saw the protesters chanting hate. Their "S's" hissed, and Tracy saw the sin consciousness that was seared onto their foreheads.

"They are not acting like Me," He explained. *"Did you ever see Me do that? They are today's Sadducees and Pharisees, and I am not in that. They are the ones forbidding to marry, and commanding to abstain from meats, not realizing that I, the creator, created marriage and food to be received with Thanksgiving. I not only created the marriage feast, I blessed it in Person!"*

A tear fell onto Tracy's cheek, and He became serious.

"But if you do not believe this truth, it will not set you free, and you will stay in bondage."

"Really Lord?"

"Yes!" He said with a great shout. *"Because every creature of God is good, and nothing is to be refused. So, I need you to receive this word with thanksgiving in your heart, because verse five is the Grace to walk in it."*

"Wow," Tracy said, and sat back to take it all in. "How many people have You shown this to Lord?"

"I have shown this to a lot of people, but they have not seen it."

Tracy wanted to receive it for himself, but was still unsure. "You need to help me out with this some more Lord," and the Lord's patience was inexhaustible.

"If I am in you," He said sweetly, *"and you are in Me, there is no escape. Could Noah fall out of the ark?"*

"No…" Tracy answered.

"Noah fell down in the ark, but he could not fall out of the ark. Noah was in Grace floating upon Grace. Therefore Tracy, you can not fall out of Me, because if you could, that would mean you would be stronger than Me, and you would be stronger than the Blood…"

And suddenly, the Tall Shiny Silver Figure became inflamed. He spread His arms like the angel when he smote the demon in Tracy's vision, and the train of His robe filled the room with glory. Without a shadow present, the Tall Shiny Silver Figure looked like He did when fighting Satan: He was Christ on the cross, and the Holy Spirit was aflame about Him. The Holy Spirit's wings were spread as a Phoenix, and there was a flame like feathers above His head. Then, Tracy was made to understand that when the Holy Spirit descended at Jesus' baptism He came as a dove, which ate worms. Now, in the end times, the Holy Spirit was a Phoenix to slay the dragon:

"…AND NOTHING IS STRONGER THAN THE BLOOD."

As quickly, the Tall Shiny Silver Figure's all-consuming light, and the Holy Spirit's fire was retracted. Then, as if blowing across a feather, the Tall Shiny Silver Figure breathed into Tracy:

"So get this revelation Tracy, and walk in it:

Galatians 3:

28 There is neither Jew nor Greek, there is neither bond nor free, there is neither male nor female: for ye are all one in Christ Jesus."

"Neither male nor female," Tracy repeated. "So you mean..?"

"This is your revelation Tracy," He said. *"Why? Because you are all one in Christ Jesus,"* and He pressed into Tracy the most and whispered. *"So, are you ready to find your perfect spouse?"*

All of a sudden, Tracy's mind was changed and the world could not tell him no. Because Tracy received his revelation with thanksgiving, he became determined. Tracy knew in his heart that he had the freedom Christ's Blood was shed for him to walk in, and the word 'wife' was no longer part of his thinking.

"*Good,*" He said. "*So, are you really ready for this?*" He repeated. "*Because I am about to shake the foundations of your world Tracy. It will blow your hair back, and it will take a while for the dust to settle. All you have to say is yes.*"

"Yes," Tracy said. But then he wanted to know.

"So, how do I find my perfect spouse Lord?" and as Tracy said it, he became lighter. "I mean, you have to tell me who the right one is, because I don't have time to pick an Ishmael. I have a bad track record in terms of my past boyfriends, as you know, otherwise I'd be happy by now."

The Tall Shiny Silver Figure's board and pointer went away. His robe became normal because the schoolmaster was finished with the law, and He looked at Tracy.

"You pick him out," Tracy said.

The Tall Shiny Silver Figure smiled because He already had, which made Tracy realize that fact.

"But how I will know who he is?" Tracy asked.

"*Do you remember when you and Tori went shopping at Pier One?*"

'Oh, here we go with Pier One again,' Tracy thought.

"*You are the one who likes that store,*" He said. But He went on, "*and I told you to buy that wrought iron artwork?*"

"Yes…"

"*And you came home, and hung it on your foyer wall?*"

"Yeah, and I hung it too close to the ceiling. I wanted to move it down to center it on the wall, but you wouldn't let me."

"*The reason I would not let you move it, is because the perfect spouse I have for you will put something beneath it.*"

"Really Lord?" and Tracy wondered what would fit there, because it was such a narrow space.

"*That is My will for you, and that will be the spouse I have chosen for you.*"

Tracy wanted to go look at the wrought iron décor hanging on the foyer wall, but He wasn't done.

"But you can not tell anyone. That is between Me and you, because if you tell someone Tracy, anyone, they will put something there, and you will have created an Ishmael."

"Yes Lord," Tracy said. "I understand. But how do I look for my perfect spouse?"

"Put an ad on the internet for the desires of your heart," He said.

Then, for the next two days, Tracy got ready for his new job, and prepared to meet his perfect spouse.

Chapter 40

- Tracy's wrought iron artwork

Tracy's first week at his new job was typical with orientation. More importantly, Tracy was free to find his perfect spouse. Several men answered his ad, and Tracy found it easy to weed through most of them conversing by email. The first person Tracy met was not a good fit, which was obvious when they got together over coffee.

The second candidate was a good match, and they dated a few times. Their careers were compatible, and he spoke of the future they could build together. He was a college quarterback, a man's man the way Moody liked Pete, and was effervescent like Justin. As time went on, Tracy was ready to place a pause on his website profile.

Before he did, Tracy decided to spend a weekend alone with God because he didn't want to run blindly into another bad relationship. Besides, there still wasn't anything under the iron décor in his foyer. On the other hand, Tracy thought, he hadn't checked his profile in a while. After work, Tracy got some dinner and decided to watch a movie. When he logged in there was a new email that seemed to fit and Tracy answered. As the conversation continued it seemed the feeling was mutual.

What are you doing tonight? the third man typed.

I am just staying home to spend some time by myself, Tracy responded, because he had purposed not to go anywhere or see anyone.

Well that's fine, I work mostly on the weekends, and I have to get up early tomorrow. Would you like to meet tomorrow night?

'That's not pushy or overly aggressive,' Tracy thought, 'and he seems genuinely interested.'

Well, I'm not going anywhere, Tracy typed, *if you want to stop by.*

I have another few students, the third man said, *and then I could come over, if that would be ok,* and it was.

Tracy met Bob late on Friday, November 10, 2006, and they watched a movie together. Bob was Tracy's age, white, and average height. He had a crew cut and wire glasses, which Tracy thought made Bob look intelligent and that he had potential. The next night, Bob came for dinner. It got late, and Bob had to get up early on Sunday to direct his church choir.

"Why don't you stay over," Tracy offered. "My house is much closer to your church, and that way you won't have to drive home. I'll make breakfast for you," and he did.

Over the next month, Tracy continued dating the second candidate, and saw more of Bob. Then, Tracy visited Bob's voice studio at his church and became more intrigued. A few weeks before Christmas Tracy had a project to finish that required him to work late, and he wouldn't get home until after dinner. It was a Tuesday, which was one of Bob's odd days off, so Bob offered to cook dinner. Because Bob had a roommate he asked to cook at the townhouse, and Tracy checked in.

'Why does he want to cook me dinner while I'm not there?' Tracy asked. 'Nobody has a key to my house. Todd doesn't. Neither does Tori, who I've known all my life.'

Tracy didn't get an answer, and understood he was on his own.

'But he does work for a church,' Tracy reasoned. 'I know where to find him. It's not like he's going anywhere, and he's been here before.'

So Tracy gave Bob the key to his perfect townhouse, and left for his long workday.

As for Bob, he had his weekly meeting with the Pastor in the morning. That was followed by rehearsal plans and edits to the church bulletin. Then Bob was free for the afternoon, and he headed to Tracy's townhouse. By mid-afternoon, Bob was at the grocery across from Tracy's development, and he went to work in his kitchen.

By evening, Bob had pâté, cornichons, Gruyere and apple slices plated on the kitchen's granite countertop. He had Parmesan encrusted pork chops holding in the oven, garlic mashed potatoes and minted baby carrots waited on the stove, and the banana pudding cooled in the refrigerator. Bob borrowed the CD player from the Jacuzzi, and set it up in the kitchen to play Mel Tormé - the 'Velvet Fog'. But nothing prepared Bob for the reception he received.

Around eight-o' clock, Tracy entered his well-lit house. When he looked at his foyer wall, Tracy slumped against the front door. He dropped his briefcase involuntarily and began to cry, which Bob didn't realize at first. Tracy couldn't move and continued to sob. When Tracy gradually slid down the door to sit on the floor, Bob became concerned. It was the first time Bob had ever been in Tracy's house by himself, and he wasn't sure what was happening.

"Are you ok?" Bob asked, but Tracy wasn't reachable.

Unknown to either of them, as Bob locked his studio door something caught his eye. Bob had all his worldly possessions in the voice studio he built off the choir room of his church. Before he left to cook Tracy dinner, Bob grabbed the framed needlepoint his grandmother had given him. It bothered Bob that the first thing seen in Tracy's home was a wrought iron décor hung too high. Bob thought there would be just enough room, and decided if Tracy didn't like it he would take it down immediately. When Bob let himself into Tracy's townhouse, the first thing he did was hang the needlepoint. To Bob's surprise, it fit perfectly between the ironwork and the light switch, and the wall seemed complete.

That was the first thing Tracy saw when he entered his perfect house, as someone stood in his kitchen. Then, what had God promised Tracy washed over him, and he was overwhelmed. All Tracy could do was look at the needlepoint underneath his wrought iron artwork that read, 'God Bless Our Home' in red letters with a pink yarn background. Bob's Mom-mom made it for him for Christmas when he graduated college, with hopes Bob would settle down and start a family.

"If you don't like the Velvet Fog, we can put on En Vogue," Bob said, but there was no response. "Is it the Gruyere?" Bob tried. "Because I know a lot of people aren't familiar, although it's a great cheese, especially with apples." Tracy kept sobbing.

'I can't believe this is him Lord,' was the only thing Tracy could think. 'How is this possible?' There was no answer from Him.

Bob came over to collect Tracy's briefcase and set it to the side. Then, he tried to help Tracy slide himself back up the door to stand. Bob knew that whatever was happening, it was cathartic. Bob also knew that Tracy, the person who had awakened more within him than he thought possible, was at a crossroads. So, Bob didn't say any more, and waited until Tracy was able to stand. After, Bob wiped Tracy's eyes with a tissue.

"I thought you liked pork chops," Bob joked, and Tracy smiled a little.

"You don't understand," Tracy said.

"That's ok. But let's get this coat off, and we can get you settled down."

"That's just it," and Tracy looked at Bob as tears ran down his face.

Bob had no idea what Tracy meant. But Bob did want Tracy to be ok that he was in his house when Tracy came home, and that he felt safe. Bob also didn't want his pork chops to dry out, so he took Tracy's coat and hung it in the hall closet. Then he helped Tracy into the kitchen, and offered him something to drink to go with the hors d'oeuvres.

"I think I need to go upstairs," Tracy said, without having anything.

"Ok," Bob said.

"And maybe I'll take a shower to get the day off," Tracy decided.

"That's fine, take your time," Bob said, and Tracy went upstairs to his bedroom. Bob turned off the oven, and went to wait on the burgundy couch and watched TV.

'Are you for real Lord?' Tracy asked, as he took off his suit and tie.

There was still no answer. The proof was on the wall, but Tracy decided not to tell Bob. The two hadn't known each other that long, and they hadn't had a chance to talk about God other than their churches. Tracy didn't want to scare Bob, so he kept what he was experiencing to himself.

Although, Tracy decided to explore the idea Bob might be his perfect spouse. A few days later, they went to a community Christmas concert. On the way home they passed Tori and Tracy's church, and Tracy decided to find out.

"So, what's you're relationship like with God?" Tracy asked.

"I'm not sure what you mean," Bob said. "Do you mean in terms of my work with the church?"

"Maybe," Tracy said. "But I was thinking of your personal relationship with Him."

"Well," and Bob had to think a moment. "I feel closest to Him through music. I feel close to God when I sing, and I always know what hymns to pick for each service before I know what the sermon is about."

"Well, that's something," Tracy said, although what Bob said didn't seem much, compared to being in His presence as often as Tracy had.

"I also know when I'm not in the right place," Bob said, "which is where I've been a lot the past few years," and Bob realized he was considerably lighter, because there was grace in Tracy that Bob hadn't experienced in many years.

"But that's how I know what to teach," Bob continued. "Whether it's a private student or my choir, something comes over me. Then I say things that are more brilliant than I understand, or, I move people emotionally before I know what I said. That's when I know He helped me unlock something. I feel His Spirit come through me, He helps the choir sing, and we inspire the congregation."

Tracy kept listening.

"I feel like a conduit when I conduct," Bob said. "It's my job to pull out the love and beauty that is inherent in the music, in order to bless the congregation with it."

"Like a connection between the two worlds," Tracy said.

"The two worlds?" Bob asked.

"Well, this world and," and Tracy hedged, "the heavens."

"That's it exactly," and Bob smiled. "I have always felt I could help people experience God through music, especially choral music, because a choir literally speaks the truth."

"I wonder," Tracy said, and then he thought, 'what are you putting together Lord?'

"What?" Bob asked. Tracy was wary, but took a step.

"I wonder if God is putting together a Praiser and a Worshiper."

"I'm not sure what that means," Bob said. "But I know our church experiences are different. I'm not very familiar with the charismatic church. I've only known 'traditional' churches. I was drawn to the National Cathedral because the music was so good."

"It is different," Tracy said, and decided to take another step. "So, have you ever heard from God?"

"You mean, heard His voice directly?"

"Yeah," Tracy said.

Bob was about to say no, but then he remembered something he hadn't thought about in decades...

Bob was born in New Jersey, but moved to Maine when he was eight. He spent his summers on Hurricane Island, where his parents worked for the Outward Bound School. He listened to readings of Thoreau and Nietzsche on the 'Morning Meeting Rock', and learned about his 'inner child'. Then, Bob had an odd experience. Hurricane Island was a marvelous but dangerous place. The purpose of the month-long course was to push students to find themselves, which included capsizing a pulling boat for safety training.

The double-ended boats were like Viking ships, and were stripped for the drills. Only the built-in rowing benches, and a small deck for the helmsman remained. In that deck was a two-foot square opening for a portable compass. The boats were wooden and heavy, and the 'Watch' of twelve college kids capsized the boat on top of them. For safety, a pair of divers was in the water. They guided students into the air pocket, or cleared them to the surface. As a teenager, Bob ran a small outboard skiff kept on standby for years. He watched boat after boat turn onto its occupants. Then, Bob heard the divers explain to panicked students how to dive back down, and get out of the air pocket under the capsized boat. The summer after his freshman year of college, Bob decided to become such a diver.

The day for his training was overcast. At first, Bob observed the two divers in his wetsuit, and his weight belt made him otherworldly in the water. Before the second capsize, Bob's instructor suggested he hold the edge of the boat as it came over. This would effortlessly push him down from the weight, and then Bob could resurface.

Because the other divers needed to be by the students, Bob did this near the stern of the boat to stay clear. What Bob or his teacher didn't realize was the eddy of the tide. In the small cove, the current's circulation was strong a few feet below the back of the boat. As the pulling boat came over, Bob put his hand up to catch the rail, which pushed him under the water as planned. When Bob thought he was in the air pocket, he hit his head. It was dark and disorienting, and he reached up and felt the flatness of plywood. Then Bob realized he had drifted up into the steering deck. So he tried to push himself down to have the tide carry him out from under the boat, but the funnel of the tide was too strong. Bob realized he was quickly running out of oxygen and options, and that he was at an unmistakable crossroads.

Then, Bob was made to understand there was air in the compass box. He reached up to feel the deck again, and found the small square hole. He put his hands in and felt air rather than cold water. At that point, Bob knew he had to trust Him more than himself. The question was whether Bob's head would fit, and if there would be enough air trapped for him to take a breath. It was also an all-or-nothing deal, because Bob knew he had to expel all his air before he ripped off his mask to breathe inside the box. Then, as Bob hung weightless three feet underwater, he felt a warmth hold him as He guided Bob under the two foot box. So, Bob exhaled all his bad air and ripped off his mask. Then he felt the shock of Maine water, tilted his head skyward and took a humongous breath into darkness.

Immediately, it was if a light was switched on. Bob saw his head inside the compass box as if he watched the scene in a movie. But it seemed to Bob he was with someone, and Bob took several breaths. His energy was replenished and then some, which made Bob laugh. Totally refreshed, Bob tilted his head to get out of the box. He inadvertently let go of his mask, and swam blind because of the salt water. But Bob knew how far to get out from under the boat, and that he had passed the test.

When Bob surfaced, he heard the other divers helping students out from under the boat's air pocket. Once everyone was out from underneath, Bob's instructor came around the stern of the boat with his mask.

"Are you ok?" his instructor asked.

"I'm great," Bob said. "I guess I lost my mask in the process. Thanks for getting it for me."

But Bob was glad he lost his mask, and from then on, he knew how much God had his back...

Now, as they drove, Bob couldn't believe he had forgotten.

"I think I did," Bob said.

"You think you did what?" Tracy asked, because a bit of time had passed during Bob's reverie of twenty years, and the revelation was strong.

"I think I have heard God," Bob realized, "although not directly, like a voice. I just felt His presence, and He showed me what to do, and He saved me."

But He wasn't done with Bob. In fact, He was just getting started.

- Mom-mom's needlepoint

Chapter 41

- Granny's Christmas, 2006

Once Tracy entertained the idea that Bob might be the one, a rapid series of events were set into motion. The first was Todd's Christmas party the following weekend. Moody's declining health subsumed most of Tracy's year. A few people knew that he had moved into his townhouse the previous January. Justin had heard Tracy had moved in with Todd, but he didn't know that Tracy had moved out, and this created a circumstance worthy of any soap opera.

When Justin called Todd to inquire about Tracy, Todd only informed Justin that Tracy wasn't there. Todd did say Tracy would be attending his Christmas party. So, Todd invited Justin to his party, but didn't tell Tracy in order to surprise Tracy. Justin had called because he was coming to D.C. for a caucus, but he had also recently broken up with his partner of fourteen years. Unbeknownst to Todd, Tracy planned to introduce Bob to some of his friends. On the night of the party, Tracy called to make sure it was ok if he brought a guest.

"Hey Tracy," Todd said. "You're coming, right?"

"Of course I am," Tracy said. "But I wanted to make sure it was cool if I brought someone."

"You know I have plenty of room. Is it Tori?" but Todd got distracted. "Move that over there. No, on the other side," and Todd came back. "Sure Tracy, I'll see you when you get here," and Todd hung up.

"What kind of party is this?" Bob asked.

"It's a Todd party," Tracy said. "You'll see."

When they pulled up to Todd's house, the red carpet went from the front door to the driveway, then down to the sidewalk for guests arriving by chauffeur. Once inside, the serpentine revolving tree of live poinsettias captured guest's attention. The next eye-catcher was the two-story Christmas tree in the living room. But every room had a tree including the garage, which was decorated with vintage matchbox cars. However, before all of that, Tracy and Bob went to sign the guest book and Todd came over.

"Hey Tracy," Todd said, and he looked at Bob.

"And this is," and Tracy thought a moment. "This is my friend, Bob."

"Well hey Bob," Todd said. "It's nice to meet you." Then Todd looked at Tracy, and cocked his head a little before he whispered in Tracy's ear. "I have a surprise for you."

"Oh?" Tracy said loudly, and looked around. "Where is it?"

"Well, 'it' will arrive shortly," Todd said, "but I didn't realize you were bringing a date."

"Did you hire a stripper?" Tracy asked coyly, although he really hoped Todd hadn't.

"You'll see," Todd said, and walked off.

"Tracy!" Sabrina yelled from the living room. "Oh my gosh, I haven't seen you in forever!" and she ran over, and practically jumped into Tracy's arms.

"Hey girl!" Tracy said. "I know I've been busy this year." Sabrina stood back to look into Tracy's eyes.

"I'm so sorry to hear about Moody," Sabrina said. "I know that must have been rough on you."

"It was," Tracy said, "but I'm here."

"Yes you are," Sabrina said, and she looked at Bob.

"And this is Bob. We met a month ago."

"Hi Bob," Sabrina said, and smiled. "It is very good to meet you," and they hugged.

"Glad to meet you too," Bob said. "I've heard stories, but it's good to actually meet you."

Sabrina laughed. "What did he say about me?"

"Nothing too incriminating," Bob admitted. "But it's clear you two go back a while, which is always a good thing."

Then Sabrina's entourage of power lesbians decided the gay boys were monopolizing too much of her time. Before they succeeded luring Sabrina back, the doorbell rang and no one answered it. Then it rang again.

"Why isn't Todd answering the door?" Tracy asked.

Sabrina shrugged. Then Todd sauntered over with a grin and looked at Tracy.

"It's for you," Todd said, and gestured toward his gránd entránce.

"Is this my surprise?" Tracy asked. "My surprise can ring the doorbell?"

Todd just smirked, before he was whisked away by the caterer for a food-related emergency.

Tracy went to the door, and wasn't sure whether the stripper would be a sailor, a cop, or a sexy black Santa. When Tracy opened the door he saw Justin, caught his breath, and promptly closed the door. Tracy hadn't seen Justin since Vera died, and the disconnect was too much for him.

'What is going on Lord?' Tracy asked, but there was no answer. Tracy realized he shut the door on his past abruptly, so he re-opened it.

"What are you doing here?" Tracy asked. Justin smiled, because he understood.

"I was in town for a meeting," Justin answered sheepishly. "I called Todd to ask about you, and he told me about the party tonight."

"Oh," Tracy said, and then Justin laid more on the line.

"I also wanted to see you," and Justin leaned into Tracy, "because I broke up with my partner."

"Oh," Tracy said, and thought of the awkward scene in "Brokeback Mountain".

"Surprise!" Todd yelled, running for Tracy. "I see you got your present. Do you want to introduce him to Bob?" Todd asked with mischief.

"Sure," Tracy said, and came back to the situation with fresh eyes.

"Bob," Tracy called, and motioned for Bob, who was still with Sabrina. "Come over here, I want you to meet someone."

Bob came over, and Tracy made the introduction by the revolving poinsettias.

"Bob," Tracy said, "this is Justin, the first guy I ever dated," and Tracy searched before he knew what to say. "Justin, this is Bob," and Tracy smiled, "my fiancé."

"What?" Bob asked.

Out of nowhere, Todd's cousin Dana came screaming on tiptoes.

"Did you say fiancé?" Dana inquired, who was obviously the most fabulous gay man in the room. "Because if you are about to be family, we need to know if we approve."

"What?" Bob asked again, but his question was obviously of no importance.

"Come with me," Dana said, and grabbed Bob's hand to drag him to Todd's office.

"Did you just say fiancé?" Bob asked.

"Yes," Tracy said, and Bob was surprised.

"Do you mean it?" Bob asked.

"I think so," Tracy answered, which was good enough for all that was going on.

"Come," Dana demanded. "You need to be interviewed," and he went down the hall waving for Bob to follow. Bob looked at Tracy.

"Dana's a good friend," Tracy said, "and he really is Todd's cousin. I've known him a long time, and he wants to get to know you because we're together."

So, Bob was fully vetted from college work experience to favorite color. Dana actually wrote things down, once he found a pen and a yellow-lined pad in Todd's desk. Later, Bob met Justin, and with Tracy the three had a good talk away from the din of the party. As time went by, Bob saw why Tracy loved Justin. Justin's memories of Vera and Moody also enlightened Bob as to who they were in Tracy's life. The next to win over was Granny.

Christmas was on a Monday, so Bob and Tracy packed up the car before they headed for Christmas Eve Service. Bob's church service started at five, would be done and dusted by six-thirty, and then they could head to West Virginia to surprise Granny. Before they went, Bob wanted to know what to get Granny for Christmas.

"Granny has everything she needs or wants," Tracy said.

"But what does she like?" Bob asked.

"You really don't need to get her anything. She won't use it, and she won't like it if you go out and buy her something."

"I can't meet your grandmother for the first time empty handed."

"Well, you've talked to her on the phone, why don't you ask her?"

"Then she'll know something's up," Bob decided.

Then, the plant in the corner caught Tracy's eye. Bob had gotten a potted Norfolk Island Pine for the dining room. It came with silver glitter and ornaments, and Bob added white lights and red bows. Bob got it as a surprise and cooked dinner again. When Tracy came home from work he was arrested again, and got a tear in his eye.

"What's wrong?" Bob asked.

"Nothing's wrong," Tracy said. "It's just that you put up a Christmas tree."

"I'm sorry, I thought you would like it," and Bob came over, and they looked at the young green tree together.

"I haven't celebrated Christmas in this house before," and then Tracy was surprised at himself. "And I haven't decorated for Christmas in years," and he looked at Bob. "My Mom died right after Christmas."

"Oh, I didn't realize," Bob said, and thought he had been insensitive.

"No, it's ok. I just hadn't thought about it. I used to love Christmas," and Tracy smiled. "Maybe it's time to change that."

"Or, maybe I should stop bringing things over here if it always makes you cry," Bob said, because Tracy still hadn't explained the significance of his Mom-mom's needlepoint.

A week later, Tracy looked at the little tree and got an idea. "Granny does like her houseplants."

"She does?" Bob asked.

"You'll see," Tracy said. "She has them in front of the windows in her living room."

"Is there a lot of light?" Tracy looked at him, because he didn't understand. "In Granny's living room, is the light the same amount as here in the dining room?"

"It's about the same," Tracy said.

"Done," Bob said.

The next day, Bob repotted a peace lily in his studio because he knew it needed more light. Then, after Christmas Eve Service, Tracy and Bob hit the road. They spent the night at a downtown Charleston hotel, and in the morning, Tracy gave Granny a call.

"Merry Christmas!" Tracy said.

"Merry Christmas to you Tracy," Granny said. "You're up early."

"Granny, you know I'm always up early. So, what are ya doin'?"

"I'm not rightly sure yet Tracy."

"Are ya dressed?" and it was hard for Tracy to hide his excitement.

"Now, why do want to know that?" and Granny paused, "but I'm not runnin' 'round the house naked, if that's what ya wanna know."

"Well, I have a surprise comin' for ya, an' I wanted to make sure."

"Tracy, I'm sittin' here in my robe an' slippers, like I have for the last fifty years."

"Ok Granny," Tracy said. "Just keep an eye out, an' have a Merry Christmas."

"Alright," Granny said, "I'll be right here. The kids aren't comin' 'til this afternoon."

After they got dressed, Tracy took Bob on a driving tour of Charleston. He mentioned the cows as they headed around the curves of the highway, which followed the Kanawha River up to Rand.

"An' there's a farm on the way to Granny's" Tracy said. "It has these cows that are black, with a big white stripe in the middle."

"You have Belted Galloways here?" Bob asked. "We called them oreo cows growing up."

"I don't know what they're called, but we have them."

"But that's impossible," Bob said. "We have them in Maine near our house, and the sign on the barn says they're the only farm in the U.S. that raises them."

"Well, you tell me," Tracy said, as they drove by the pasture full of Belted Galloways.

"Yep," Bob said. "Those are oreo cows."

Then, Tracy and Bob realized both of their high school's colors were blue and gold, and their mascot was the panther. They both played various brass instruments at basketball games in band, and both wore a banded collared shirt for their senior picture. As they meandered through Rand, Tracy pointed out his schools, the little church he went with Aunt Z, and the community center.

Finally, they drove down Starling Drive to Granny's house. Bob stayed close behind Tracy as they went up the walk, even as Bob carried the large peace lily between them. Granny opened the front door as they got to it.

"I thought ya might be doin' this," Granny said. Tracy gave her a big hug. Then Granny stood back, and Tracy stepped aside to reveal Bob.

"An' this must be Bob," Granny decided with an odd smile, "with a plant." Granny looked at Bob more to study him, except the plant was in her way.

"This is for you," Bob said, but to Granny, that was obvious.

"Well," Tracy said, "let's put this in the living room," and he grabbed the plant.

"Yeah Trace," Granny said, "just put it over there somewhere," and she pointed absently as she looked at Bob fully. "Now, come on in here an' give me hug."

Then, Bob spent the rest of the day meeting most of Tracy's 'runnin' cousins'. He met Marie, who lived down the street, and had a little boy and girl in elementary school. Demi had driven up from Charlotte with her boy and girl. Mia's three boys were there, although she was with her husband's family in Kentucky. So, kids from three to eighteen arrived mid-afternoon with lots of funny stories about Granny. But most stories were about Moody, because it was the family's first Christmas without him.

After opening presents, the group sat on the large sectional sofa until they spilled into the large space in front. They all had a memory, and everyone had a tear to shed about something Moody said or did that changed their life. Bob was also moved, because even though he was the only one in the room who wasn't family, he was completely welcomed, and made to feel as familiar as Granny's furniture.

"How about the two dollar bills?" Tracy asked. "It didn't matter what time of day or night, or where ya were, Moody could pull a two dollar bill out of his pocket."

Everybody talked at once about how many they had gotten in birthday cards, or found hidden in a present they wouldn't find until they got home. Then, Marie got a big grin on her face.

"Y'all know why Moody always had two dollar bills, don't ya?" Marie asked.

Everyone's expression went blank except Granny's, but she didn't say anything.

"No, why?" Tracy asked, and Marie looked directly at Granny.

"Well, Moody told me you always thought it was the devil's money," Marie stated. "So, he kept buying the bank out of two dollar bills, 'cause you wouldn't touch 'em."

Granny looked forward as if she wasn't being addressed, but Marie continued with her indictment.

"An' then, Moody said as time went by, an' you saw all us kids were able to spend 'em, you wouldn't use 'em out of spite. That way, he could keep some cash on himself."

Everyone looked at Granny.

"Huh," was all Granny said, and the family laughed until it hurt.

- Tracy and Marie

- Mia with her beer

Chapter 42

The next day, Bob and Tracy left Rand for the townhouse so they could repack. Because they had the week off, the new couple decided to continue introducing each other to their families. On Wednesday, they hopped a plane to visit Bob's family, who lived in the mid-coast region of Maine. Compared to West Virginia Maine was colder, but for Tracy it was the darkness that was astounding. It was pitch black outside by the time the "Oprah Winfrey Show" aired at four-o'clock, and there were other stark contrasts to the Christmas at Granny's.

Bob's grandfather had passed a few years before at ninety-five. A little before Christmas, it was necessary for Bob's parents to put his Mom-mom into assisted living. Bob's younger brother was in Egypt, serving in the Army Reserves. He had recently divorced, and his young kids were with their mother's family. Over the past two years, Bob's older brother had come out, divorced his wife and moved in with his partner, which made Christmas anything but traditional for the family.

Where the two-story great room once held uncles, aunts, cousins, and great-grandchildren vying for space around Pop-pop's recliner, there was a vast emptiness. The huge Christmas tree usually stuffed with ornaments from Bob's great-grandmother's flower shop lay cold in the basement. Bob's parents were shell-shocked, as they still took care of Bob's fifty-six-year-old Down-Syndrome uncle. They tried to keep the status quo, but the new reality couldn't be avoided.

Now, Bob's parents sat with their two gay sons and their new partners - who had somehow replaced their parents, daughters-in-law and grandchildren, and any familiar memory of Christmas. Yet the small group had a good time - although dinner was like a scene from any movie where the history of the room was much too big for the disjointed guests left at the table.

When they got back home, Bob and Tracy's family introductions were done with one exception. Then, once again, Tracy's father dropped in unexpectedly. It was now March, and Harry called to let Tracy know that his Great Uncle Bob had died.

"Are you going to the funeral?" Tracy asked.

"Yes," Harry said, and he was solemn. "Your Mom and I are going. It's this Saturday."

"I'll meet you there," Tracy said. "I have someone I want you to meet," and Harry took that in. "Are you going to be ok Dad?"

"Yeah son," Harry said. "I'll be alright. I'll see you there."

On Friday night, Tracy and Bob drove to West Virginia and stayed at Granny's house in Tracy's room. The next morning as Bob got dressed, Tracy went in for another cup of coffee. From Tracy's expression, Granny knew it was the two of them that had to 'have a meetin'.

"What's wrong Tracy?" Granny asked.

"Granny," Tracy said. "I'm concerned about Dad meeting Bob."

"Why's that?"

"Well, Dad an' I never really had the conversation," and Tracy paused. "It's always been implied, an' we've prayed against it. Now, I have a new revelation about that, an' I've been set free."

Granny turned to look at Tracy.

"I can see that," Granny said, and got quite serious. "I wasn't sure the first time I met Bob. Moody died recently, an' you coulda still been in your euphoria about a new relationship. So I was concerned whether you were gonna make it through that patch. But now that I'm seein' Bob a second time, an' seein' you again, I'm ok, because I know you're ok."

Tracy could hardly believe it, and just looked at Granny.

"I was really concerned," Granny said. "But now I see you're gonna be ok, an' we *all* like Bob."

With that statement, Tracy knew that meant everybody – Jinny, Alvin, his cousins, and everyone in the little neighborhood of Rand.

Then, Granny grabbed a knife off the kitchen counter, pointed it at an imagined foe and her voice went hard.

"An' if your father don't like him, then he can kiss my ass. An' you can tell him I said so."

Tracy smiled for a variety of reasons, but Granny wasn't done.

"We like Bob," Granny established. "He brought me a plant."

Tracy had to laugh.

"Now go on an' get yourself dressed," Granny said, "so you won't be late."

So the two left for the funeral in their suits, and Bob had his first real taste of West Virginia. Uncle Bob's church was up in a 'holler' - but not like the swale that held the street between Granny and William Russell's house. This was a dead-end holler with hairpin turns, which required the Subaru be downshifted into first gear.

When they reached the tiny white church, it was cantilevered from the mountain. The back of the church nuzzled into the slope, and the entrance steps dangled over fallen rocks at a forty-five degree angle. It was also apparent steel beams weren't considered, because of the long cracks in the cement block foundation. As Granny predicted, Bob and Tracy were late and the service had started. After they scaled the loose shale to the front steps, they entered the small vestibule. Every seat was taken in the wooden pews that held about fifty.

Because the church doors were open to the sanctuary, Tracy and Bob stayed put. As they did, a few congregants turned to see who came in. Bob realized he was the only white person there. Although that wasn't uncomfortable, because he had often been in such circumstance. The unnerving part was adding the weight of two people to the unbalanced end of the church. Bob had already visualized the church breaking loose and skiing down the mountain, as in any scene from the "Pirates of the Caribbean" franchise.

Yet Bob was comforted when the choir entered. Tracy already mentioned that Great Uncle Bob was a person of stature in height, width and depth, and the fact his oversized casket was directly underneath the narrow stage for the minister was a relief. However, after seven women of like stature entered in oversized robes, and stood behind the minister to sing their choir selection, Bob breathed a little easier. Then Bob wondered.

"Where are your parents?" Bob asked in a whisper.

"Do you see the tallest head," Tracy hushed. "Right in front of the casket on the left side of the aisle? And do you see the carefully combed hair of the woman sitting to his left?"

Bob looked. "You mean the man in the handsome suit, and the woman in the fire-engine red jacket?"

"That's them," Tracy confirmed, and Bob had to stifle a laugh.

"What?" Tracy asked.

"I'll tell you later," Bob decided.

Tracy looked at him. They were in the vestibule, and no one could really hear them.

"Ok," Bob whispered. "Do you remember me telling you about my best friend Jim, even though he's forty years older?"

"Your professor at Ithaca?" Tracy asked.

"Yeah, who taught me how to do the Madrigal Feasts. Anyway, he had a lot of colorful expressions, because he was originally from Fort Deposit, Alabama."

Tracy had no idea what this had to do with anything.

"So, that's your step-mom up there, right?" Bob asked. "The one in the red?"

"Yup," Tracy said, "although I just call her Mom, and she only wears St. John, so that is a top-of-the-line wool suit."

"Well that may be," Bob said, "but I know what my good friend James Edward would say."

"What would he say?" Tracy asked, and he thought he was ready. But Bob pulled out a perfectly bent southern accent that would have made Lady T blush:

"Honey, there are only two kinds of women that should wear red, and she is not a Spanish dancer."

Tracy took it in for a moment. Then, he emitted a high-pitched squeal, stomped the floor with his size-thirteen dress shoe, and immediately ducked down. Not knowing any better, Bob stayed standing in the middle of the vestibule. The very black West Virginian congregation turned around and saw Bob, who looked back at them like a D.C. albino deer in headlights. Then, the congregation looked at each other to see if anyone knew Bob. They wondered if the little white boy was lost, or whether he meant to laugh at an extremely revered black man's funeral. They also considered whether Bob would fit next to Uncle Bob in his casket, if it were necessary to hide the body.

Tracy realized Bob needed to be claimed, so he grabbed Bob's hand and told him to get down.

"What are you doing?" Bob whispered.

Tracy still had a scene from the inverse version of "Get Out" playing in his mind, but quickly stood to the amazement of the back half of the congregation.

"Come on let's go," Tracy said, hearing banjo music, and he dragged Bob out of the church, and down the loose shale to the car where they could safely laugh their asses off.

After the funeral, Tracy and Bob followed the procession down the holler, across the highway that split Charleston, and onto the opposite high ridge. It was threatening to rain, but the view was breathtaking down the long curved valley of the Kanawha River. The gravesite service was short, and because there were fewer people Bob got to have a look at Tracy's parents. Harry and Lynn also saw Tracy. Afterward, Harry came over and gave Tracy a hug.

"I've missed you son," Harry said.

"I've missed you too Dad," Tracy said, and they separated. "Dad, I want you to meet Bob," and Tracy presented Bob in such a way that Harry knew who he was.

Harry reached out his hand, and Bob could clearly read Harry's first, middle and last name embroidered on his cuff, which was something Bob had never seen before.

"Hello," Harry said in his trademark way, and they shook hands.

"It's nice to meet you," Bob said. Then he stepped back, because he was the stranger at a funeral.

"Where are you two staying?" Harry asked Tracy.

"We're staying at Granny's," Tracy said. Harry raised an eyebrow.

"Really?" Harry asked. "And what does Granny say about that?"

"Actually," Tracy replied, "she told me tell you that we *all* like Bob."

Harry's eyebrows went higher and then, Lynn finished her conversation with a relative and came over.

"Who is this Harry?" Lynn asked quickly, referring to Bob.

"Hey Mom," Tracy said, and they hugged before Harry continued.

"Honey, this is Tracy's friend Bob," Harry said. "Bob, this is my wife Lynn."

"Nice to meet you," Bob said, and shook Lynn's black leather glove.

Lynn smiled back, and Bob went back to stand by Tracy.

"Honey," Lynn said quietly and to the side. "What is this?"

"Later," Harry said softly, "but Granny says we *all* like Bob."

"Oh," Lynn said, and began to process what that meant. Then Harry and Lynn had to get back to Ohio, so they said their goodbyes.

After that, Bob and Tracy were off to Mia's. She was having the family over for dinner to watch a bootlegged Pacquiao fight. Because Mia was away for Christmas Bob hadn't met her, even though he met her three sons. This made Tracy realize something as they drove up the steep holler to her house.

"Now I haven't mentioned this before," Tracy said, "but all the women in my family have a switch."

"A switch?" Bob asked.

"Yeah. I didn't know about it until Marie explained it to me. But they all have a trigger, and Mia's is the worst. So, if you see her get a strange look in her eye, or she says something strange, just give me a yell."

"A yell?" Bob asked, as they pulled up to the house.

"You'll be fine," Tracy said. Then he jumped out of the Subaru and ran into the house to see everybody, but mostly because of the height issue with Mia's house.

Bob lagged behind, because he was taken that Mia's house was situated the exact opposite of the little white church from that morning. This holler was just as steep, but it was the road that clung to the mountain. From the road's edge, Mia's house had two steep steps down followed by a small bridge, and somehow, the house clung to the mountain without tumbling into the gorge and small stream a hundred feet below. Fortunately it was getting dark, so Bob was able to get to the front door before vertigo set in.

Once inside, the small living room opened to a large, dimly lit dining room. There steam pans hissed full of fried chicken, collards, corn bread and mac and cheese. Granny put down her chicken wing and came over.

"How'd it go?" Granny asked at point-blank range.

"It was good," Tracy said, but Granny didn't stand down. "Really, I think they like Bob too."

"Huh," Granny said, and went back to her fried chicken.

Tracy re-introduced Bob to the group from Christmas, and they all said, 'We all know Bob,' who smiled because he was old news.

"Well I don't know no Bob," Mia said, with a tilt of her head.

Tracy went over to his cousin for a hug. Mia's husband filled the doorframe from the kitchen, who had been a professional football player before his shoulder had trouble.

"Yeah," he said. "Where's this 'Bob' we've been hearin' so much about?"

Bob was introduced, and learned more about Tracy's family. The first lesson was how to drink beer.

"Here ya go Bob," Mia said, and she handed him a can. "You wanna straw?"

"A straw?" Bob asked, and Mia showed him the bendy straw sticking out of her twenty-ounce.

"It get's ya there faster," Mia winked.

Then she walked into the dining room drinking her beer like a sippy cup. And she was right about the straw, because a little while later Mia was on a roll.

"Oh yeah," Mia said. "You ain't gonna find me gropin' around tryin' to find no bat. That's why I got my pool balls lined up."

"What is she talking about?" Bob asked Tracy, but Mia heard him.

"What?" and Mia turned and asked Bob. "You don't have protection?" and Bob's mind went immediately to condoms, and somehow Mia read his mind.

"An' I'm not talkin' about no condoms," Mia confirmed. "Although, they're in the same drawer right next to my pool balls. No, I mean if a woman is alone in the house, an' ya hear somebody bumblin' around downstairs, ya don't have no time to be searchin' around for no baseball bat, that coulda rolled too far under the bed."

"That's right girl," Marie agreed.

"No, you need somethin' ya can put your hands on," Mia said.

Bob looked at Tracy, but he just grinned.

"You don't believe me?" Mia asked. "I'll show ya. I'll be right back."

Mia went upstairs, opened the drawer to her nightstand and came back. What she had in her hand was a white gym sock with red stripes. Two pool balls were obviously stuffed into the toe, and the sock was stretched to the point it looked like it needed a truss.

"That's what I'm talkin' about," Marie said.

"An' if you whip this thing around, you can crack a skull," Mia said, and she started slinging her sock, but her husband ran over as if he had a flashback.

"Easy girl," he said. "We're all family here," and took the loaded sock from his wife. Then everyone had some dessert. But as the evening progressed, things got more dangerous than Bob anticipated.

Granny and Marie went home. Just Tracy and Bob, Mia, her husband, and her teenage boys got ready to watch the boxing match. For some reason, Bob ended up on one of the two gray velour loveseats in the tiny living room. Bob sat on a loveseat on one wall, and Mia sat on the other. Then Mia got a strange look, even though Bob had been there for over four hours.

Tracy was in the kitchen talking with Mia's husband. Mia cued the fight, and the announcers discussed Pacquiao. Mia didn't say anything, and Bob stared blankly at the TV. Mia sipped her twenty-ounce through her straw and took a sideways look at Bob, who pretended to watch the TV. Bob snuck a peak back, and Mia quickly stared at the screen. Then Mia looked at Bob again, and cocked her head as she sipped her beer loudly through her straw. When Bob looked back, Mia snapped back to the TV, and this happened a few more times before she spoke.

"Now, I know I should know this," Mia said, and took a long slurp. "An' I don't mean to be rude or nothin', but who are you, and what the hell are ya doin' in my house?"

Bob didn't wait for the pool balls. Instead, he recognized the switch and yelled, "Tracy!?!"

- Granny's squirrel lunch

Chapter 43

But the family introductions didn't stop. In April, Bobby's father died. Tracy's Bob went to the funeral, and met some of Tracy's cousins from that branch of his past. Tracy hadn't seen them since Freddie died. Bob also met David, who happened to live a stone's throw from the townhouse. So, in less than six months since Bob hung his Mom-mom's needlepoint on the wall, everyone knew the phrase 'Bob and Tracy'. Then, the pair went to Granny's for Mother's Day to surprise her again. Tracy called her on the way.

"Hey Granny," Tracy said. "What are ya doin'?"

"Thinkin' you're up to somethin'," Granny said. "You comin' this way?"

"Well," and Tracy laughed, "Bob an' I are half-way there to see ya."

"What time?" Granny asked.

"A few hours," Tracy said. "Do you want us to stop for some chicken? We can get a bucket of extra crispy on the way."

"Actually," Granny said, "I had a couple of squirrel defrostin' from the freezer. Ask Bob if he's had any squirrel," and Tracy saw the look on Bob's face.

"I don't think he has Granny," Tracy said.

Bob shook his head no.

"Well, I think it's about high time he had," Granny said. "I only had three left. But I'll get William Russell to shoot another couple off the wire."

"It's no problem to stop and get some fried chicken Granny," Bob offered.

"I don't want ya to go to any trouble," Granny said, and she was on a mission now. "What time you say you'd be here?"

"By lunchtime," Tracy affirmed.

"Ok," Granny said. "I'll be ready," and she was.

Granny had her cast iron skillet piping hot when Bob and Tracy walked through the door, and the squirrel was almost done. Then Granny had to make the squirrel gravy.

"This is the best part," Granny said, and she was right.

Bob thought squirrel tasted exactly as one would expect – hyperactive and like acorns. However, squirrel gravy was pretty good smothered over white bread, and Bob tried to eat another piece. Because the animal was small, the only thing edible was the legs. To Bob, once the legs were splayed and smashed flat to fry, it seemed clear he was eating squirrel ass.

When Tracy spit something out that made a 'ting' on his plate, Bob was done.

"What's that?" Bob asked.

"Oh," Tracy said. "I forgot to tell you to be careful of the lead pellet," and he put the small ball of lead on Granny's Formica table.

The pellet rolled off onto a tall stack of newspapers sitting on the chair next to Bob. When Bob picked up it up, he noticed the manila envelope it fell on. The envelope had "The Will" handwritten on the top two corners, which was underlined twice.

"Oh my goodness!" Bob said.

Tracy looked at him, and Bob picked up the important looking envelope.

"Shouldn't this be somewhere else?" Bob asked.

"That's just recyclin' I been savin'," Granny said.

"Granny?" Tracy asked. "What's going on?"

"There's nothin' goin' on," Granny said, "because there's nothin' in there."

Bob looked, and there wasn't. Granny looked at Tracy squarely.

"Now you know," Granny said, "Moody always wanted you to have the farm."

"I thought so too Granny," Tracy said, "although, he never said it outright."

"But when it all came down to it," and Granny was vague, which even Bob picked up on, because Granny was never vague. "There wasn't anything to it," and for the moment, that was that.

By the end of the month, Bob and Tracy were back in Rand for Memorial Day. The pair went with the family to decorate graves at various cemeteries, and Granny showed Bob where she was going into the ground. Recently, Granny had a cataract removed so she had to wear large sunglasses. Bob dubbed them her 'rock star glasses'. Granny immediately adopted the nomenclature because by this time, Bob liked Granny as much as Granny liked Bob. They made each other laugh constantly, because of the way they each turned a phrase.

Then, Bob decided Granny needed something pretty to look at when she was done with her sunglasses. So, when Tracy took Granny for her check-up, Bob started digging next to her sidewalk. Granny's hostas were choked with grass, and Bob moved them under the oaks on the side of her yard. Then Bob began in earnest, preparing the rocky ground for a rose bed to line Granny's walk.

The first gun-related incident happened when Miss Mary pulled into her drive. Miss Mary lived two houses down, and was a seemingly sweet, plump-faced white woman. As Bob found out later, Granny said she had a good side and a bad side.

"You gotta watch Miss Mary," Granny said. "The bad side is klepto, an' the good side is paralyzed," and both things were true.

As Bob was about to experience, Miss Mary had obviously had a stroke, which was why she was running around town in her minivan. Later, Tracy corroborated about the kleptomania.

"She seems innocent enough," Tracy said. "Then I gave her a ride back from church one day. She thanked me for the ride, and positioned herself to get out on the passenger's side. Then she swiped every pen an' piece of change I had in the middle console before she left out an' slammed the door."

At the moment, Miss Mary pulled into her driveway, which was on Granny's side of her house. She pulled into the hill to her basement garage, and was eye-level with the ground. Then she rolled down her car window, and took a closer look at the white man digging up Granny's yard. It was a hot day without any wind, and Bob had been at it for a while. By this time, Bob had also hung out with Tracy and his 'sister-cousins' enough to pick up some syntax. Unfortunately, Bob had never even heard of Miss Mary.

"Where's Jackie?" Miss Mary asked roughly.

Bob looked over, and eventually found the eyes that peered up from the ground two yards over. The only problem was that Bob didn't know where 'Jackie' was. Bob only knew Granny, and had never heard anyone call Granny by her first name. So, Bob assumed the woman was addressing someone else and didn't answer. Miss Mary became concerned.

"Where the hell is Jackie!?!" Miss Mary demanded. When Bob realized he was the one being yelled at, he decided to 'go Granny Moody on her ass'.

"Who wants to know?" Bob yelled back, which was all Miss Mary needed to hear.

Miss Mary slammed her minivan in reverse, and 'squealed tires' out of her driveway. She continued backwards up the road past the entrance to Granny's driveway, and then 'squealed tires' until she was even with Bob and slammed on the brakes. Then, Miss Mary narrowed her eyes at Bob, who stood ten feet from her with his pickax, and she put her car in park. Miss Mary studied him again before deciding to go for her glove box, and Bob realized things were getting serious.

"I don't know where Jackie is," Bob explained. "But Granny is with Tracy at her eye doctor's appointment."

Miss Mary put her revolver back in her glove box, and turned to look at Bob with an odd smile. "So, what's you're name?" she asked.

"Bob," Bob said, and the good half of Miss Mary's face lit up.

"So you're Bob," Mary said sweetly, which was quite a switch. "Jackie didn't tell me Tracy was comin' to town."

"She didn't know," Bob explained, "because we surprised her. That's why we're moving her hostas and putting in a rose bed – to surprise her."

"Well, if that isn't just the sweetest thing!" and now Miss Mary was almost Bob's next of kin. "I've heard a lot about you, an' we're so glad Tracy finally found someone."

Bob didn't know what to say to that.

"We're all just so pleased," Miss Mary said sweetly, immensely pleased with herself. "So you just carry on. An' don't forget to drink your water. It's a warm one."

Then Miss Marry reversed gently out of Granny's driveway, and returned to her driveway without telling Bob her name. Later, Granny figured out it was 'Klepto Mary' that almost mowed Bob down on her front lawn, and they were introduced. The day after, Bob almost shot himself helping turn Granny's mattress. No one told Bob about the rusty ax and loaded pistol Granny kept under her pillow.

When Bob got there first to remove the bedding, he jumped back before the gun went off. However, Bob and Tracy put in Granny's roses without further skirmish. The pair headed back to the townhouse and then, at long last, the final series of events were set into motion.

Back in January, Tracy quit his job at DC Metro after he was almost in a knife fight with a deranged lunatic. Tracy had gone out to get coffee for everyone. When he came back, Tracy wondered why police officers and dogs had surrounded the building. No one said anything as Tracy swiped his ID card, rebalanced his macchiatos, and headed for the Accounting Department where he worked. When Tracy went to open the door, it was locked. He looked through the wire-reinforced window, and his co-workers were nowhere to be seen. When Tracy knocked, everyone's head popped out from under their desks.

"It's Tramele," they said in hushed tones. "Should we let him in?"

"Hey guys," Tracy said. "What's goin' on?"

"Shhhh," everyone said. Then a brave soul came and opened the door for him, shuttled him in, and quickly locked the door again.

As it turned out, someone was running around the building with a knife, trying to steal the payroll that was in a large safe two doors down. That was enough for Tracy. When he came home, Tracy re-enacted the incident for Bob in front of the fireplace.

"They let me in the building," Tracy said. "They let me come all the way up all those steps - all the while knowing everything was on lockdown? An' they don't offer health insurance until I work there for a year?" and Tracy had made up his mind: "Girl, bye."

So, Tracy ended his contract and quickly found another. Then, spring turned into summer. Soon, Tracy's ninety-day contract was over the day before the Fourth of July holiday, and Tracy checked in for his next move.

"Ok Lord," Tracy said. "Where am I supposed to look for the next contract?"

He answered immediately:

"Take Bob out for a bike ride for his birthday."

To Tracy, this made less sense than usual. Tracy was also surprised to hear from Him, because Tracy had been on radio silence since he met Bob back in November.

"Lord," Tracy said. "I ask You for a job, and You want me to go on a bike ride?"

"Take Bob out for a bike ride for his birthday," He repeated rapidly.

"But that makes no kind of sense," Tracy said.

Then Tracy remembered the waterbed, desk, and other things He asked of Tracy that didn't make sense, but made faith. Although, Bob had gotten a bike before the couple met, which inspired Tracy to get one. They bought a roof rack for the Subaru, and got a yearlong pass for the Maryland Parks system. Bob and Tracy enjoyed how other Subarus with bikes on their roof honked their horns at them. When they passed each other, Bob and Tracy would shout in unison:

"We got bikes!" and they pumped their fists and said, "Yeah!"

So the Lord's request wasn't totally from left field, but Tracy felt a sense of urgency. Since Tracy met Bob nine months earlier, Tracy's life events seemed to be speeding up. Tracy felt like he was going somewhere, which he was. In fact, the Lord's plan involved flinging him into an unknown farther than Tracy could imagine, and the arc of his life was about to have a landing point.

But at this moment, Tracy became pragmatic.

"When is Bob's birthday?" Tracy asked, but He was too excited to be specific.

"Go now," He said.

"Now?" Tracy asked.

"Now," He repeated, and the Tall Shiny Silver Figure's exhilaration was reminiscent of the first time Tracy met Him when he was three.

"Where should we go?" Tracy asked.

"Go to the other side," He answered quickly.

Tracy understood that meant across the water, which from the townhouse meant the Eastern Shore of Maryland. So the next morning, Tracy called their lesbian friends.

Rae and Kate had met shortly before Bob and Tracy did. The two couples were almost identical, except for their opposite sexuality. Rae had sung in Bob's church choir for years, and Bob knew Rae's girls since they were tiny. Once Rae finally came out, Bob was her support system when Rae found Kate. Soon after, Kate became the other pea in the pod for Tracy.

The upshot was that Bob and Tracy's 'lesbian wives' naturally had more camping equipment than any gay man could possibly need or want. When the Tall Shiny Silver Figure told Tracy to 'go to the other side', they were Tracy's first call for help, which they answered with gusto. So by late morning, Bob and Tracy had the necessary equipment to head to the Eastern Shore. Tracy planned to use their park pass to go camping, and the culminating journey was begun.

- Kate and Rae with Tracy and Bob

Chapter 44

- the radar station

By the afternoon of July 5, 2007, Bob and Tracy were headed across the Chesapeake Bay Bridge from Annapolis. Tracy was instructed to 'go to the other side', but He wasn't more specific than that, and the Delmarva Peninsula was more than one hundred miles long in Maryland alone. Tracy's plan was to go to a state park near Crisfield. He had researched it the night before, and the park honored their pass. However, Tracy still hadn't told Bob anything about his relationship with the Tall Shiny Silver Figure, which made things vague as far as Bob was concerned.

"So," Bob asked. "Where are we going?"

"I told you," Tracy said. "We're gonna celebrate your birthday."

"Ok," Bob said.

In the past, Bob was the one who did such things for others. Now that the shoe was on the other foot, he realized how it might be more fun for the person orchestrating the surprise.

"I've been to Rehoboth Beach," Bob said, "and that's a nice place."

But Tracy drove through the intersection that turned east to the ocean, and kept heading south.

"You'll see," Tracy said, but he was flying as blind as Bob.

Eventually, the pair made their way to Janes Island State Park, and it was close to four-o'clock. They found where the campsites were, and pulled the Subaru into a sandy space under forty-foot loblolly pines. Tracy pulled out the abused box of tent parts Rae and Kate gave them, none of which made any sense. Their lesbian cohorts actually gave them two tents, which could be constructed with a living room, sleeping quarters, and possibly a gallery. But the two gay boys couldn't make heads or tails of it, and there were no instructions.

"Do you think they have cabins?" Bob asked.

It was now late afternoon, the sun was headed toward the horizon, and mosquitoes were gathering.

"Let's check," Tracy said immediately.

The couple headed to the ranger's office, and Bob noticed that the map on the wall of the building was actually a chart. Then he noticed the racks of canoes and kayaks stacked by the launch area, and the small inlet that separated them from a pristine island of pines.

"Hey Tracy," Bob said. "Look at this."

Tracy came over.

"These aren't bike trails," Bob explained. "They're kayak trails through the marsh."

"What?" Tracy asked, and was annoyed.

"See?" Bob said. "The trails are only one or two miles long, and they're blue. I like canoeing, but I haven't spent much time in a kayak."

"Aw hell no," Tracy said, who instantly heard the theme music from "Jaws" mixed with the banjos in "Deliverance", and he was losing his patience. "Let's just see if we can get a place to stay."

Bob and Tracy headed to the door of the ranger's office, but it was locked. When they looked through the window, the ranger was at her register counting the drawer. They knocked, but when the ranger saw them, she motioned that the office was closed.

"We were just wondering if you had any cabins available for tonight," Bob said through the glass.

Then, when the ranger came over to the door, a remarkable thing happened. She didn't say anything, instead, she pulled the shade down over the window - so the ranger literally kept the door shut, and fully closed the window in front of Bob and Tracy's face.

"Let's get something to eat," Tracy said testily.

The couple repacked the mangled tent parts into the Subaru, and headed back to civilization. By this time, Bob knew Tracy loved soft-shelled crabs. Crisfield, Maryland, was famous for the delicacy, and they headed to a restaurant that was supposed to be the oldest and best. What they got from the huge steamer on the slow night were tiny purplish-red rocks. They resembled crabs only by the fact they had two melted claw appendages jutting from them, and they were inedible.

"Come on," Tracy said. "Let's go," and he was more than miffed.

They hopped back in the car to steam back home. Bob knew not to say anything, and had no idea what was going on. Tracy didn't either.

'What's going on Lord?' Tracy fumed. 'You're the one who told me to 'go to the other side'. Here we are, and nothing is working.'

There was no answer, and Tracy thought he missed God. There was something he wasn't getting, and nothing made any sense. After they had been on the road an hour-and-a-half, it was close to eleven-o'clock. Bob wasn't having much fun on his 'birthday trip', and he saw a sign for St Michaels.

"My parents used to talk about St Michaels," Bob said.

"What?" Tracy asked absent-mindedly.

"After my parents married, they came to St Michaels a few times. This was long before they had us, and we moved to Maine. My Mom used to tell stories of 'the town that fooled the British', and the Cannon Ball House," and they passed a highway sign informing them

St Michaels was ten miles away.

"Do you want to go there?" Tracy asked.

"It's pretty late," Bob said, "and you have been driving all day."

"Well," Tracy said. "That sounds like a good idea," because he was tired, and was at the end of his rope.

So they went to St Michaels, pulled into the motel, and Tracy collapsed. Before Bob went to sleep, he went back to the lobby for information about the area. There, a skipjack brochure caught his eye. Bob grew up in a boatyard, and his family moved to Maine because of his 'sister' - a Friendship Sloop built in 1902. The Rebecca T. Ruark was a local skipjack built in 1886, and was similar to the wooden sailboat of Bob's childhood. He thought it might be fun to sail on it with Tracy. Then, Bob went back to their room, climbed in bed and went to sleep. The next morning Tracy woke up, and asked the same thing he did every morning.

"What are we going to do today Lord?"

"Why not wait for Bob to wake up and ask him?" He said.

"Why do we have to wait for Bob to wake up?" Tracy asked indignantly. "You didn't even tell him I don't have a job."

There was no answer, so when Bob woke up Tracy asked him.

"Do you know there's an island farther down the road?" Bob asked, and Tracy waited to see what Bob would say. "Well, I saw a brochure for an old sailboat that does tours, and since today is my birthday,"

"Today is your birthday!?!" Tracy interrupted.

"Yeah, so, I thought it might be fun to go on a boat ride,"

"Wait," Tracy interjected. "Today is your birthday, not yesterday?" and Bob nodded yes. "Oh wow! So I didn't miss God!" and Tracy was ecstatic.

So Bob made the call, and they found out the skipjack was booked for the afternoon. But they could go on the sunset sail at six-thirty, although it was a long time to wait.

"Are you sure you don't want to go back home?" Bob asked. "Because I know you're tired."

"No, no, no," Tracy insisted, and his mood had changed significantly. "*Today* is your birthday."

"Ok," Bob said, "but it always has been," because Bob had no idea why this was so important. "Why don't we go down to the island and look around."

"That sound like an idea," Tracy said, who was now letting Bob lead.

Then they headed to Tilghman Island where the skipjack was docked, and ate at a restaurant on the Narrows by the drawbridge. After lunch, Bob and Tracy hopped back in the Subaru to explore the island. This didn't take long, because the island was basically a single road that dead-ended into a huge parking lot. They parked and got out to look at the Chesapeake Bay, but they still had another three hours until the sailboat cruise.

"So," and Bob looked around. "Do you want to get the bikes down and ride around?"

"Sure," Tracy said, who didn't think much of it. He was too distracted by the large fenced-in area with a three-story tower, which somehow looked connected to Area 51.

There was a radar station at the end of the huge parking lot, and there were no cars or other signs of life. After he read the sign, Bob found out it was the first erected at the end of World War II to test radar equipment. The naval radar lab was across the bay. The station communicated with the lab for radar testing, as well as monitored boat traffic going in and out of Baltimore.

However, all Tracy saw was a military installation. He was concerned about his security clearance, and Tracy's résumé was already circulating for his next contract. He didn't want to have to explain anything to his new employer, so he was wary.

"Do you have the keys?" Bob asked, and Tracy handed him his keychain to unlock the bike rack.

Then, Tracy stalled getting his bike off the car as he considered the radar station. Bob had his bike together, and was soon riding around the parking lot. Bob looked farther down the road and saw a sign for a bed and breakfast, and rode back to report his findings.

"Hey Tracy," Bob said. "There's an Inn past the radar station. Do you want to check it out?"

"That looks private," Tracy decided, "so we probably shouldn't go down there."

"How can an Inn be private, if there's a sign advertising it's down the road?" Tracy didn't answer.

Bob was weary of how arduous his 'birthday surprise' had been to this point. So Bob went down to the gate this time, and read the sign about the bird sanctuary and the Inn. Beyond the gate, the road turned to gravel. There was a sharp turn to the left, which revealed a grand expanse of water. In the distance was a tilted lighthouse in the middle of the bay, which the land had abandoned decades ago. Bob became intrigued, and he rode back again to tell Tracy.

"This Inn seems like it's beautiful, and the view is fascinating,"

"I really don't think we should go down there," Tracy said, who had suddenly returned to the mood of the previous day, and Bob decided he had had enough.

"Well, it's my birthday," Bob stated. "So I am going to go see what I can see," and he took off on his bike past the radar station, rode through the gate, and went down the gravel road until he rounded the corner out of sight.

"Lord," Tracy said, and he was furious. "Bob just took off through that gate, and he has my car keys."

His answer was immediate. *"What did I tell you to do?"* He asked.

At first, Tracy was perplexed. Then Tracy remembered His instructions.

"You told me to take Bob out for a bike ride for his birthday," Tracy recited.

"Well," He said. *"This is Bob's birthday, and this is Bob's bike ride. . . "* and Tracy felt a smile from Him that was unusual... *"I suggest you follow him."*

Tracy grudgingly mounted his bike and rode through the parking lot, but he stopped at the corner of the radar station. He dismounted in front of the government-issued barbed wire fence, took his wallet out, and held it against the crystalline blue sky reflecting off the Chesapeake Bay.

"Lord," Tracy declared, "if I lose my security clearance because of this stupid bike ride; You, me, and Moses are gonna sit down an' have a conversation."

Then, Tracy pushed his wallet back into his pocket and aggressively rode down the gravel driveway to get his keys. But the driveway was a half-mile long. It meandered along the marsh to Tracy's left, and there were open miles of water to the right. Along the length of the shore was a carefully angled bank of ton-sized granite boulders known as riprap.

To Bob, who grew up on an island that had been a granite quarry, he felt at home in a way he never had in Maryland. Because it was the end of the peninsula, the vista also looked like where Bob grew up in Penobscot Bay. The view fascinated him to the point he had to dismount his bike at the top of the lawn in front of the Inn. Bob stood there, entranced by the fact someone had put Maine smack-dab in the middle of the Chesapeake. Tracy caught up to him, but before Tracy could demand his keys back, an older man came from what looked to be the service-entrance past the front door of the old house.

"What are you two guys doing here?" he asked, and it was hard to decipher whether his manner was just gruff, or sardonic. "Do you have a reservation?"

When the man came for them, he walked with a swagger that meant he owned the place. He had carefully combed black hair, which obviously lost the battle with the wind constantly. He had a barrel chest, was energetic, and there might have been a twinkle in his eye that suggested good humor. However, at the moment, the man was Tracy's worst nightmare. He was sure all the man saw was the interracial gay boys that had invaded his private sanctuary, and Tracy was sure naval officials had already been notified to take them away to the brig.

"I'm sorry sir," Tracy said. "If we were trespassing we do apologize. We were just out on a bike ride, and we stumbled upon this place."

"Are you two looking for a room?" the Innkeeper asked.

"Well," and Tracy finally looked around. "What is this place?"

"We're a bed and breakfast," the Innkeeper said.

Bob looked at Tracy, because he didn't understand his nervousness.

"Well," Tracy said, "we have plans to go on a sunset sail this evening."

"On the skipjack?" the Innkeeper asked. "You'll have a good time with the captain. He's a trip."

"Yes," and Tracy relaxed and looked at Bob. "And I'm sure we don't want to drive all the way back home afterwards."

Bob nodded in the affirmative.

"So sure. Why not?" Tracy decided.

Then, Tracy silently unpacked a litany of how he could keep his security clearance, even though the room probably cost more than he wanted to spend. It was paramount for Tracy to keep what God had given him since his Mom died, and staying here meant he could protect his work experience, from nuclear inspection, to requesting his own teams as an independent consultant for Oracle contracts...

"I tell you what," the Innkeeper said.

"What?" Tracy asked, because his entire work-life, and what God had brought him through to this point had just passed from beginning to end in front of his mind.

"Lean your bikes up against that big holly tree over there," and the Innkeeper pointed. "Then, take a walk down to the dock. By the time you get back, I'll be finished cleaning up breakfast."

"Ok," Tracy said.

Bob was delighted but stayed clear, because his birthday surprise was finally getting somewhere.

"Then, you can meet me in the office," the Innkeeper said. "I'll have the paperwork ready, and you can rent that last cabin for the weekend."

"For the weekend?" Tracy asked.

"Well, it's Friday," the Innkeeper said, who was a consummate salesman. "By the way, my name is Tom."

They shook hands, and Tom went back into the house. Bob and Tracy leaned their bikes against the trunk of the immense holly tree by the office, and they headed for the dock.

"This is where you are supposed to live," He said, and He was beaming. But as the couple continued down the rounded driveway to the back cove, Tracy began to wrestle with God.

'Newsflash Lord,' Tracy thought. 'I don't have a job to afford all this,' and then Tracy thought that was a little harsh. 'But, if this is you Lord, confirm it,' although Tracy still couldn't believe it. 'But if this is you Satan, I bind you according to Matthew 18:18, and I loose you from your assignment against me this day,' and Tracy bowed his head and said aloud, "in Jesus' name."

"What?" Bob asked, but Tracy didn't reply.

As they reached the dock, both were affected as the events of two lifetimes unfolded. In a one-dimensional way, Bob was like a fish to water. As he walked down the dock, Bob heard the waves washing up into the crevices of granite boulders - a sound he hadn't heard since he was a boy on the island. For Tracy, reaching the dock was the culmination of two worlds, and, unbeknownst to Tracy, a bridge was about to be crossed at the all-important page of his picture book, and Bob would confirm this.

Chapter 45

- the back dock

Bob and Tracy walked down the long dock. Bob looked over the broad expanse where the Choptank River met the Chesapeake Bay. Tracy peered over the end to see how deep it was, and did a necessary scan for shark fins. Tracy also pondered His last statement, which was, 'This is where you are supposed to live.' As Tracy thought it, Bob was in hysterics.

"I just heard from God!" Bob shouted, "and He said this is where we are supposed to live!" Immediately, Tracy thought he should test that spirit and faced Bob squarely.

"Oh, you mean rent that cabin for the weekend?" Tracy asked quickly. "Because that's exactly what we're going to do. We're going to go back up to the office, give Tom my credit card, and rent that cabin for the weekend," and Tracy turned to look across the river.

'This isn't fair Lord,' Tracy said to himself. 'I've only known Bob for nine months.'

"You said it yourself Tracy," He said. *"Remember? Back in Ohio?"* and He quoted Tracy: *"If a woman can birth something in the natural in nine months, surely You can birth something in the supernatural."*

Tracy pondered that statement for a split second, before Bob became dogmatic. Bob stomped his feet and pumped his arms for emphasis like a child.

"No Tracy," Bob decreed. "I did just hear from God, and He also told me to tell you to look!" and Bob's arm went up of its own volition.

Unknown to Bob, he pointed to the most southern end of the island. From the end of the dock, a very large cross was clearly visible. This was also the vantage point from which Tracy 'painted the vision and made it plain' in the sixth grade. This moment was also the first time Tracy saw the cross since being on the property. Upon seeing it, Tracy was pulled out of his body.

Immediately, Tracy was in what he recognized as the realm of his own three-year-old existence. He was in the hospital room, and watched his three-year-old self about to be put into the ice water. However, now, adult Tracy hovered in the air much like Scrooge, except there wasn't a spirit beside him as a guide. Instead, Tracy received a revelation that time was a series of frames, which he didn't yet fully understand. What was brought to Tracy's remembrance was from Hebrews 11:3:

"³ Through faith we understand that the worlds were framed by the word of God, so that things which are seen were not made of things which do appear."

This understanding unfolded as Tracy hovered in the hospital room. He watched his three-year-old self fight the doctor, so he wouldn't be put into the ice water. He watched Moody reach for 'his boy' with tears in his eyes. The Tall Shiny Silver Figure stood behind Moody with His hand outstretched. But looking at the scene as an adult, Tracy's emotions got the better of him. Because Moody had become Tracy's best friend in this world, he wanted his three-year-old self to go to Moody instead of the Tall Shiny Silver Figure.

"Don't talk to strangers," Tracy cried to the three-year-old.

To his surprise, three-year-old Tracy paused time and yelled, "Stop!" Then little Tracy looked up at adult Tracy and said, "You cannot change the decisions we have made."

The scene was now framed: the doctor held Tracy as a toddler above the white basin, and Moody and the Tall Shiny Silver Figure stood on the other side.

"You are only here to understand why we made these decisions," the toddler Tracy explained, "and remember what we are supposed to do going forward. So ask questions, so you can understand what we are supposed to do next," and then the three-year-old spoke to Tracy in an excited whisper.

"Because we're about to see the book, and we haven't seen the book since I was in the hospital," and Tracy's toddler self smiled broadly at adult Tracy. "It has wonderful pictures in it, and He's about to let us see it again." Then three-year-old Tracy instructed adult Tracy, and addressed him by his name in the realm they were in. "Now ask questions Forty-one, so we can see every detail in the book," little Tracy said.

Tracy now knew the toddler's name was Three, which made everything so much easier. It was also revealed to Forty-one that Three was instructing him how to operate in this realm of existence, because Three was the closest in age to when they first saw the picture book.

"But don't get distracted," Three said. "We have a very unique opportunity to go back and see the picture book, which not everybody gets. Most get distracted by the beauty of heaven, and they get so distracted, they don't want to leave."

That statement made Forty-one think of Lucille, Harry's mother. She was so tired, she didn't want to leave heaven to say goodbye to Harry, the son who carried the blessing that had gotten them this far.

"Don't waste this moment smelling the flowers," Three said again. "They will always be there. They are part of creation. So don't marvel at creation – seek the Creator."

As Three spoke, Forty-one realized Three was just one of more Selves he could meet, who could help guide all of them to their purpose.

"That's why we are here," Three confirmed. "To learn more," and Three turned back into his frame of time. "Ask questions," Three reminded. Then, the toddler looked back at Moody and the Tall Shiny Silver Figure to choose, and a manner of time resumed between Forty-one's questions…

"Why do we go to the Tall Shiny Silver Figure?" adult Tracy asked.

"Because He looks like what our imaginary friend sounds like," Three answered.

"Oh," and Forty-one remembered thinking that.

"Pay attention Tracy," Three reminded again. "And you are going to have to ask better questions if we're going to get any further," which made Tracy think of Peter at the transfiguration, blurting out how he wanted to build Moses, Elijah and the Christ booths. God had to tell Peter to shut up and listen to His Son. But then, Three became so excited he had to whisper again.

"We're getting ready to go," and Three reached his hand out to Him, and He took the child's hand! Then they were instantly warm and well…

But unlike what Tracy experienced when he was a toddler, Three sat on the Tall Shiny Silver Figure's lap, and Forty-one stood behind the Tall Shiny Silver Figure's chair. Forty-one looked over His shoulder, and He showed both of them the wonder…

"I want to show you some things," the Tall Shiny Silver Figure said, and he spoke very fast. Then their book was open to them and Three was delighted, exactly as he was when he first saw the book.

When they saw the page of Vera grabbing Three under her arm, and racing to Freddie's grandparent's house in a panic about 'the man who asked Tracy about the 'love walk', all of them laughed. Tracy also smelled his Mom from her holding him under her arm, a fragrance he hadn't experienced in decades.

Then, the Tall Shiny Silver Figure separated Himself from Himself, which He could do infinitely. As He kept showing Three the picture book, from His loins up, the Tall Shiny Silver Figure turned in His chair to look behind at Forty-one.

"Do you have any questions?" He asked.

"Why did Your voice change when I came back from sitting in Your lap?" Forty-one asked.

"Because you grew up in Me," the Tall Shiny Silver Figure answered, and they went back to look at the picture book.

Then, Forty-one-year-old Tracy realized he could go further. Tracy understood that he could study the déjà vu moments in his picture book past his present age, and that he could review them to prepare.

When the Tall Shiny Silver Figure heard that, He fully separated from Himself. He stood beside Forty-one as His other Self stayed with Three. Then, Tracy looked through his picture book past the age of Forty-one.

"Tell me about this chapter," Tracy said. "The Key, the Door, the Room, and the Table," and the Tall Shiny Silver Figure looked at Tracy with the most joy Tracy had ever seen Him have.

"It is interesting you would catch that." He said. *"Are you going to ask about the chair?"*

"The chair?" Tracy asked.

"Oh yes," He said. *"The chair activates everything."*

"What do you mean?"

"You can not get there unless you are seated and resting," He stated. *"The chair is actually the key, and the key is the access,"* and He paused for Tracy to absorb that information.

"So, now that you have access," and He smiled, *"which was because you asked…"* and He winked, *"because asking is the access…"* and Tracy understood that all of those words were synonymous.

Then He took Tracy up two steps, because the Kingdom of God wasn't far away. Tracy was expecting a giant escalator, or an endless ladder from the Old Covenant. But the journey to heaven was nowhere near as dramatic. Tracy simply turned to his left, took two comfortable steps up, and Tracy stood in front of what he knew was his door. The endless hallway was white, and all of the numerous doors seemed the same.

"Oh," Tracy said, "this looks like what Mom went through."

The door looked exactly like the one Tracy saw in the vision of the hospital with the partying imps, when Vera stood before her door at the top of the staircase, before she was taken up by His hands.

"The doors are identical," He confirmed. *"Beyond each door is unique to each individual. Your mother went to her room. But you have to ask permission to go into another's room, because you only have access to your own,"* so Tracy stopped wondering where his mother's door was. *"But I am here to show you your room, because you have to walk in this dual citizenship."*

Tracy stood on the threshold, and checked to see if Three was ok. Of course he was more than fine, sitting on His lap, enjoying the wonders of the picture book.

"I am with you always," the Tall Shiny Silver Figure explained, which Tracy understood more deeply.

The Lord was not only with Tracy in the present, He was with him in the past, and would be with him in the future simultaneously. Then Tracy took a step toward his door, and it opened like the pneumatic doors on the "Starship Enterprise", just as he hoped. Tracy also knew the door opened because it knew him.

When Tracy stepped into his room it was all white – the walls, the single chair, and the long table that stretched the length of the narrow space. There were no windows, only a single doorframe at the far end to the left. His room wasn't what Tracy expected, but with great aplomb, the Tall Shiny Silver Figure spread His arms in a grand gesture.

"Ta-da," He said, and was immensely pleased.

Tracy heard Granny say, 'Fix your face Tracy,' which he did, because Tracy expected many rooms, marvelous furnishings, and exquisite music akin to the images in the picture book. Instead, Tracy 'heard crickets' in the incredibly austere, long white empty room. Then Tracy was honest.

"What's so fabulous about this?" Tracy asked. "I was expecting a mansion."

Immediately, He was in Tracy's face: *"Many people do, but they are the ones who have to decorate their room,"* and Tracy understood the term 'decorate' was unlimited. *"One could have many mansions, or this one simple room,"* He explained. *"It depends on what you ask for. . . "*

"You have not, because you ask not," Tracy recited.

"Exactly," the Tall Shiny Silver Figure said.

They stood just inside the door. The chair was in front of them before the long narrow table, and the lesson Tracy was about to learn was important for both worlds.

"Just as you have to be seated and at rest in order to get to your room," He revealed, *"once you get here, you have to be seated at your table in order to activate it. Otherwise, it is just a blank room. Nothing will respond to you. What you see here right now is what a lot of people have on earth. They must get beyond that and start asking Me for what they want, because My Blood paid for them to do that. Once they are in their room, they have to keep asking,"* and He looked at Tracy and smiled. *"You have been decorating your room for a while."*

"How come it looks blank?" Tracy asked, and He was more pleased.

"It is blank because you did not sit in your chair to activate it." He answered. *"It is no different than putting your key into the lock of the door to your house on earth. Then you go inside, take off your coat, sit down on the couch, and grab the remote that activates 'your room'. From that point, you can put the remote down anytime you want, or get up for a snack, but your room will be activated until you leave."*

Tracy understood the remote as the way to activate the lights, TV, and stereo system in his living room at the townhouse. But he was unclear how his pristine, white heavenly room correlated, so the Tall Shiny Silver Figure answered.

"Have a seat," He said.

As soon as Tracy went to sit, his chair pulled out, and then pushed itself underneath him as he sat. Then, a smorgasbord of food came alive on the table like at Thanksgiving. Simultaneously, lights and colors of all description decked the walls with fixtures, shelves, draperies and ornaments. Exquisite music played, and doors appeared that joined to Tracy's other rooms, which Tracy knew could be infinite – room after room.

But in this moment, the large picture frames were most fascinating. They were rainbow colored, and danced as a multifaceted prism. Within each frame were what looked like tall thin strips of beveled glass, except they were slices of time captured in light. Similar to an accordion bellows, as Tracy approached, scenes from when he was eighteen expanded in order from his birthday on April 10th until April 9th the following year. Each frame was a different year of his life, and each bevel showed his life events in chronological order. As Tracy passed by a frame, that particular year of his life fanned out before him between the bevels. Then, it was revealed that Tracy could go into each bevel, and he could experience that moment of twelve, or twenty-five, or thirty-three again - the same way Tracy experienced Three before he was shone the picture book. Then, Tracy knew that he needed to understand more.

"You mentioned a remote," Tracy said.

"Go back and sit down," He said, *"or it will not work."*

Tracy immediately went back to his chair and sat down. He looked for his remote on the table, but there was only the plethora of food. Tracy noticed the food was just past his reach, and smiled in the knowledge he wasn't to reach for it. That would be considered work, which wasn't allowed in such a place of rest. In heaven, 'work' was speaking, which Tracy had learned from his lessons about speaking in tongues. But on earth, Tracy used his tongue to defeat demons. Now that Tracy was in heaven, his speech was something he wasn't sure how to operate.

"So where's my remote?" Tracy asked.

"What do you want?" He asked.

"I don't understand."

"The remote is in your mouth Tracy. Here, you really do speak and call things that be not as though they were, and then, they will be as soon as you speak them."

Tracy still didn't understand, so the Tall Shiny Silver Figure prompted Tracy to the next revelation.

"Now," He said, *"as apposed to yesterday or tomorrow,"* which He said as a joke. *"Now it will work,"* and He looked at Tracy with anticipation. *"Right now,"* and He smiled. *"Now what do you want?"*

So Tracy focused on 'now faith', and Tracy wanted his remote, because he understood his remote operated everything.

"I want my remote," Tracy said, in order to make it appear.

Immediately, the doorframe in the far left corner opened a door, and a tuxedoed butler came through the opening and stopped. He stood with His feet together at the end of the long narrow table, and held a small tray. On it was a goblet and small plate.

Then the butler walked around the end of the table and up the length, but He didn't say anything. The butler acknowledged the Tall Shiny Silver Figure with a wink as He passed, and placed what Tracy recognized as communion elements within his reach, and instantly, Tracy understood:

Tracy knew his request had to go through the New Covenant to be approved, which the Tall Shiny Silver Figure had paid for. Tracy also knew that the butler was the Holy Spirit, and that He was here to take Tracy's order after he took communion. Further, as Tracy looked at the plate and the goblet, he understood the communion elements in heaven were God's Word and the Joy of the Covenant.

So, Tracy took communion as the Tall Shiny Silver Figure and Holy Spirit looked on. Then, Tracy knew to make his request, and he asked for what he figured was the wisest thing.

"I want continual visits," Tracy stated, which made Both smile as parents would.

"That is a given," the Tall Shiny Silver Figure said. *"Because once you have received this revelation about communion, you can visit anytime you want - as often as you do this…"* and Tracy understood. *"So ask for something else,"* He said, and it seemed He wanted to give Tracy another level of Grace, but Tracy could only think of one thing.

"Just keep talking to me?" Tracy asked, as if searching for the correct answer, and He smiled radiantly.

"Not only will I keep talking to you, I will talk to everyone who catches this revelation," the Tall Shiny Silver Figure answered.

Then the Holy Spirit took the tray. Tracy remained seated as He went down the length of the room, around the end of the table, and left through the door. Tracy knew that from that point on, he could come back to his table at anytime. Tracy was also made to understand the Lord showed him his room for two reasons. First, communion in his room was necessary for him to go forward, and second, Tracy had to sit at his table in heaven and say yes, because he was about to say yes on earth.

Chapter 46

- the cross

After communion, Tracy and the Tall Shiny Silver Figure left his room. Then, Forty-one went back to look over His shoulder, and He and Three looked at the all-important page in the picture book.

"Remember this!" He exclaimed emphatically, and He laughed and bounced little Tracy on His knee. The music from the page was exquisite as He held the book up with amazement. Then He said it again with ultimate exuberance.

"Remember this Tracy. Just get here!" and He was practically dancing. *"Whatever you do, just get here,"* and His breath was caught with relief.

"Just get here, and I will come and see you again!" He said. *"When you see this again in real life, I will come back and visit you. If you say yes, I will take over your life, and we will have a really good time. Just make it to this Tracy… Just make it to this Tracy…"* and He turned to Forty-one and said: *"This is that…"* and Tracy was gently placed back into his forty-one year old body with a quiet whisper… *"this is that…"*

"No Tracy," Bob decreed. "I did just hear from God, and He told me to tell you to look!" and Bob's arm went up of its own volition.

Then, it was revealed to Tracy that he was trained to deal with this transfer between worlds. Tracy remembered the time he was driving his team in the rental car. He stopped at the red light, and the angel grabbed him to show him the zoetrope of images he was about to visit in Europe.

When Tracy was returned to his body, he was literally jolted. As he sat with his foot on the break in this world, Tracy's entire body was tensed as with an electric shock, and the last thing he wanted to be doing was driving a car. However, because Tracy sat behind the wheel, he was forced to navigate the physical world, immediately after being in the supernatural. When he was returned, even though Tracy's body was foreign to him, he had to concentrate to operate his limbs, calm his grip on the steering wheel, and feel the brake before the light turned green.

"Yes Tracy," He confirmed. *"You are a dual citizen, designed to operate equally in both worlds at will."*

"Are you ok?" Bob asked. Tracy looked beyond Bob as if he saw through him, and then Bob noticed. "You smell funny," and Tracy came back to this to world fully.

"You smell that too?" Tracy asked. Tracy picked up his collar with both hands to smell his shirt. He inhaled deeply to get as much of it as he could, and his eyes welled with tears from the essence he hadn't experienced in eighteen years.

"Yeah," Bob said, and smelled the same thing as strongly. "What is that?"

"That's Bootsie," Tracy said, "my Mom," and Tracy saw into the frame, and the moment in time recorded by the beveled glass as clear as he was standing on the dock.

"She just picked me up out of the doorway," Tracy said, "and ran across the street with me under her arm when I was three."

Bob looked at Tracy with wonder in his eyes.

"I can't explain it," Tracy said, because he couldn't begin to explain anything he had just experienced.

Instead, Tracy turned away from Bob, and he threw it right back on Him. 'Lord,' Tracy thought. 'I don't understand what just happened. I smell Mom all over me.'

That wasn't answered. Instead, Tracy kept smelling his collar to hold onto the scent of Vera as long as possible. Then, he looked over the broad expanse of the river to the south. When Tracy saw the cross again, he remembered:

"When you see this again in real life, I will come back and visit you."

As Tracy saw the cross that he drew in the sixth grade for the first time in 'real life', which was now at the end of the point, Tracy knew he had arrived at a set time. He was at an orchestrated crossroads, and this was the moment of impact. This was the predetermined point in time when the natural collides with the supernatural – this was that. Tracy also understood from recently sitting at his table, that if he recognized the impact prior to it happening he could take advantage of it, which was why Tracy was shown his room.

But Bob knew none of this, and was ecstatic as they left the dock. He literally ran circles around Tracy, bouncing up and down like a cartoon character.

"I just heard from God! I just heard from God! I just heard from God!" Bob yelled, because he had never experienced Him so directly, and the presence of His voice alone was more than he could handle.

To Tracy, Bob was more annoying than Freddie ever was, and he knew he had to stay focused. Tracy knew his emotions could sidetrack him, just like Three said. Tracy didn't want to get stuck in the mud anymore, and wanted to see the supernatural done in the natural. Tracy also understood that what was about to happen was a make or break moment. Although, if the Tall Shiny Silver Figure orchestrated it, Tracy knew He would carry him through it. So, the couple walked back up the curved drive to the office, Bob skipping and laughing, and Tracy in a deep well of preparation.

'Lord,' Tracy thought. 'I don't understand all of what just happened, but I am taking my 'butt' out of the way so you can bless me.' Then Tracy looked around, and turned in a circle pointing both his index fingers in every direction as he turned.

"This is where we're supposed to live!" Bob sang, and did another circle around Tracy. Tracy kept turning and pointing, and Tracy recognized the two of them as a wheel in the middle of a wheel.

'But if You want to love me this much,' Tracy added, 'don't let me stop You, just help me receive it.'

"*Alright,*" He said. "*Because you asked like that, I will confirm it for you one more time. But this time, when I do, write it down.*"

"What do you want me to write down Lord?" Tracy asked.

"*I will tell you what to write down, and when to write it,*" He said.

'Fine by me,' Tracy thought with the sarcasm of this world. 'Remember, I don't have a job no way. I've got nothing to lose. I'm just on a bike ride. Besides…' and Tracy became bewildered…

As he went, Tracy realized his entire body felt like when he painted the vision in the sixth grade. Tracy had experienced the same tingle when He took possession of his arm to draw the flowing wheat grass, except now, Tracy's entire being was quivering. He experienced an alert sense of awareness that was not his own, as if he was inside a bubble looking out. Anything that wanted to come into his bubble had to come through a force field of angels who were continually vigilant. As Tracy felt their alert presence, he visualized a peace he had not known before, and it was easier for Tracy to connect his déjà vu moments.

'This is the time You spoke about,' Tracy thought, 'when You told me that one day You would take over my life, and that we would have a really good time.'

"*Yes Tracy,*" He said warmly. "*You are almost there.*"

As Tracy pondered that, he had another revelation. 'You've been talking to me an awful lot lately,' Tracy noticed, and He smiled.

"I need you to tell My people that their parents were not the first ones to invent the 'Hot/Cold' game," He said. *"As My people get closer to their Promised Land, I will direct them the same way,"* and the Tall Shiny Silver Figure could hardly contain Himself. *"You are almost there,"* He whispered, and Tracy opened the door to the office.

"Welcome gentlemen," the Innkeeper said, and peered over his wire reading glasses. Tom sat in a large black office chair, behind a tall white counter and long homemade desk. His chair could face the computer cabinet to his right, or swivel to face guests entering the office, so Tom remained seated when Bob and Tracy walked in.

"I see you didn't let the cross scare you," Tom said.

"Yeah," Bob said. "What is that for?"

"We have cross burnings every Thursday night," Tom said with a straight face.

Immediately, Tracy recognized the offense before the blessing, and decided to neutralize it.

"And a barbeque on Saturdays, I hope," Tracy quipped, "because if so, count me in as grill master," which made Tom look over his glasses again.

"That was pretty good," Tom noted, "and you were quick with that. I think you're going to have a good time while you're here," and he handed Tracy the paperwork to rent the last cabin, and Tracy gave him his card.

"After this is over with," Tom continued, "let's sit down and have a drink on the back porch."

The boys thought it was a little early, but liked the idea. Tom handed Tracy the receipt on the counter. As soon as he signed, Tom swapped the receipt for the keys in a simultaneous action from his chair. Then he launched into his check-in speech.

"Now gentlemen," Tom said. "The big key goes to the padlock on the gate, and the small key goes to your cabin. Parking is on the left side past the office, and the driveway is one way. Remember that, because it pisses me off when people can't figure out how to read the giant 'One Way' sign posted in front of the house. And mind your speed, because it's a driveway, not a highway. Breakfast is eight to ten in the main house, and we lock the gate at five-o'clock," and Tom looked over the top rim of his glasses. "And make sure no one piggybacks behind you when you open and relock the gate, because I'm tired of chasing people out of here," and Tom paused.

Tracy noticed that Tom was interrupted, and had a bewildered look on his face. Then, Tom tilted his head to the side, and Tom looked off in the distance before he leaned forward and said,

"Do you guys want to buy this place?"

Instantly Time Stopped

A doorframe of light appeared behind Tom. At first, Tracy thought it was the door to the backroom, except it was much taller. But, rather than opening as a single door, the way it had behind Moody before Tracy was about to be put into the ice water, this door kept opening. At first, it opened like French doors. Then, the doorway opened as a curtain to an immense stage, and Tracy was at the center.

From Tracy's perspective, what was revealed was row after row of clouded balconies with people peering over them. Similar to a stadium, except it was in the dimensions of heaven, thousands upon thousands of witnesses appeared decked in special attire. Their rows made a grand coliseum, only this time Tracy noticed the hats the witnesses wore were unique to each individual. Each hat had a feather that shimmered with iridescent rainbow colors intermittently, which was how they communicated.

Then, it was revealed to Tracy to understand each person's feather as a flame, and was reminded of the feathers that had appeared above the Holy Spirit as a Phoenix. Then, Tracy understood the flames were how each witness was 'made to know, even as also they were known'.

This wasn't to say the stacked clouds of witnesses were quiet - far from it. The roaring cheers of the vast assembly engulfed Tracy. They were wild as they toasted each other, before joy was refilled from the bottom of their goblets. They slurred and stammered, completely drunk in the Spirit. Front and center were Tracy's familiar cheering section. He recognized Moody, Freddie, Vera, and Granny Berger, even though their heavenly bodies were at the sum peaks of their lives, and they were as care free as butterflies.

"You made it brother!" Freddie hollered.

"Hallelujah!" Granny Berger shouted. "I've been prayin' for this day."

"I love you honey!" Vera screamed, and when she waved, a unified cheer erupted from the crowd. Moody beamed, and then Freddie spilled joy all over him. Moody laughed when he went to brush it off his new clothes, except it disappeared before he had a chance.

All of this was overwhelming for Tracy, who knew not to let his emotions get the better of him. Without an outlet, all Tracy could do was run back and forth in front of the long white counter of the office. Tracy looked for an exit on stage left, and ran to the other end to escape stage right, but he was trapped in the moment of his appointed time. His stage was set, and Tracy felt like the grand prizewinner as more and more rows of clouds billowed behind another, higher and higher. More witnesses appeared in astonishingly brilliant multicolored attire, and were even more absurdly drunk in the Spirit. Then, out from behind Tom's chair, the Tall Shiny Silver Figure popped out to Tracy's right. He stood and spread His arms with an excited shout, and He sounded like a game show host.

"Tracy! I have been waiting for you to get here since..." and He pulled up His left sleeve to reveal what looked like a wristwatch...

…and Tracy marveled at the time piece, because a holographic image shown above it. The universe spun backwards above the watch, which narrowed to the solar system, and then down to earth, and zoomed in on the United States to West Virginia. Then, Tracy saw scenes of his life flip backwards to when he was three years old and in the hospital room, which was when He yelled…

"*…you were three years old! Wow!*" He exclaimed, as if completely amazed.

But everything Tracy was experiencing made his flesh want to run for the hills, so He added, "*Oh yes, peace.*"

Tracy instantly calmed down, and all manner of disbelief and unease left him.

"*I should have said that first,*" He said apologetically.

Tracy stood in His presence, as Tracy had so many times before in his life, but this wasn't a vision, this was on earth. In addition, the multitude of witnesses not only sparkled - they made a sound like a drone buzzing with excitement as the Tall Shiny Silver Figure spoke. Not only that, with so many people watching so excellently dressed, Tracy felt naked. Before Tracy could say they were a distraction, the Tall Shiny Silver Figure turned and faced the multitude.

"*Ok, ok,*" the Tall Shiny Silver Figure said, and He raised His arms as a fifth-grade teacher would in front of an excited class on a field trip. "*You are only here to be a witness,*" He announced with love.

With those words there was a hush - although it was interrupted by drunken giggles, and intermittent shouts of 'Tracy!' and, 'He's finally here!' across the breadth of the arena. The humongous crowd settled down, and only sipped their goblets of joy. Then, Tracy finally had the wherewithal to turn to Bob.

"Bob," Tracy said. "Bob, do you see this?" and Tracy waved his hand in front of his face. But there wasn't a blink. Bob and Tom were frozen in mid-breath, and He turned from the crowds to face Tracy.

"*Tracy,*" He said. "*I stopped time so we could have this conversation. No one can see or hear us but you."*

Tracy realized the word 'us' included the throng of witnesses, which seemed ironic by an earthly standard, but appropriate for the immense, opulent grandeur of His Grace.

"All you have to do is say yes Tracy," as He stated before, *"and I will take over your life from here,"* and He smiled, *"and we will have a really good time."*

Then, He looked at Tracy the way He did when they discussed 'now faith', when Tracy had sat at his table in his room before Tracy took communion with the Holy Spirit.

"This is that," He repeated with expectancy.

The many clouds of witnesses paused. Suddenly, you could hear a pin drop except for the collective understanding of the theme from "Jeopardy" that played in everyone's mind before time would be up, and it was Tracy's choice if he didn't have enough faith to take on what the Lord had for him…

"Yes," Tracy stated.

The clouds and clouds went wild with cheers. Yet above the frenzy, Tracy could hear Vera, Freddie, and Moody scream with abandon. But Granny Berger couldn't contain herself, because she not only loved "Jeopardy", her great grandson answered correctly!

"You go boy!" Granny Berger yelled at the top of her new lungs.

Then, the Tall Shiny Silver Figure hunkered down like a football linebacker and Tracy was the quarterback, and Tracy got scared.

'I ain't never played football,' Tracy thought. 'That was Freddie, who only did it to meet girls…'

"I did not ask you all that," He said quickly, and did not change His stance.

So, Tracy thought he was about to be squashed by an overabundance of love. Instead, His right arm extended from His body, which was followed by His hand and index finger that stretched until it hovered above the guest book on the counter in front of Tracy.

"Write this down," He instructed. Then He looked into Tracy's eyes, and He quoted without the use of speech: *"...and to whom is the arm of the Lord revealed?"* as His finger touched the guest book. He continued to communicate with His eyes, and the Tall Shiny Silver Figure downloaded future events into Tracy, as He moved from His stance to catch up with His finger.

As He got closer, the pupils in the Lord's eyes turned to a flame, which Tracy recognized as his own reflection, but was actually the image of the Holy Spirit within himself.

"Is that how You see me?" Tracy marveled.

The Tall Shiny Silver Figure was immensely pleased, and Tracy realized how he was transforming Grace upon Grace. Then, He walked through Tom, through the desk and counter, and toward the door behind Tracy. Yet His index finger never left the guest book, and His eyes never left Tracy's gaze.

But everything else of the office became translucent as He walked out the door, and His elongated arm kept His finger on the guest book. Then, He began to float upward, and a cloud enveloped the Tall Shiny Silver Figure. As He rose, the cloud descended the length of His arm to His hand, and when the sleeve of the cloud reached His fingertip, it was retracted from the page and time instantly resumed.

"Do you guys want to buy this place?" Tom asked, and Bob gasped.

Tracy stared behind Tom, because the entire host of witnesses had disappeared, which left an amazing void. Tracy did have the presence of mind to remember His last instruction, which was 'write this down'. Tracy wrote his name, Bob's name, and then wrote the address to the townhouse, his email address...

'You're not saying anything Lord,' Tracy thought. 'I have seen and experienced too much today not to believe what I saw. I experienced time repeating itself, flipping through the pages of my book backwards, and a gazillion people goading me on. Not to mention Mom, who I smelled here in this realm,' and Tracy was determined. 'So, I will doodle all over this page for a year…'

As soon as Tracy committed himself, and purposed his flesh to stand in that moment without saying another word until the Tall Shiny Silver Figure answered, instantly, Tracy heard Him, and he wrote it down:

"B.T.W. Owners Don't Sign The Guess Book. Happy Birthday Bob."

'Oh,' Tracy realized. 'I misspelled the word guest. Should I cross it out?'

"No Tracy," He said. *"Guess what I am about to do next."*

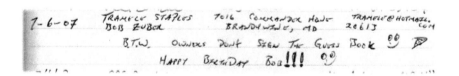

Afterwards

Cue Music: To be read hearing "Walking on Sunshine" by Katrina & The Waves...

Bob read over Tracy's shoulder and told Tom that 'owners don't sign the guest book', so they were going to buy the Inn. Bob and Tracy's first morning on the point was July 7th of 2007, or 07-07-07.

However, that took three years. Every morning by His instruction, Bob and Tracy sat on the front steps of the townhouse, pointed east and said, 'Black Walnut Point Inn, come to us now'. In the meantime, He prepared them. Bob learned what Tracy had experienced with Him, was born again, and on June 6, 2010, the 'Secret Place of Peace' was moved from Lot 91 to the end point of Tilghman Island.

The following summer, Granny came to visit the Inn she had heard about for three years. Being from the mountains she wondered, 'How high does that water get?' However, she was delighted, and saw all that the Lord had done for Tracy before she went to be with Him the following year.

Then Bob and Tracy set about transforming the Inn. They offered a Sanctuary Discount, and began planting gardens according to what seed He showed them to put in the ground. As with all things with Him, everything increased, and over the years Black Walnut Point Inn became a haven where the most usual statement from guests was, 'Heaven on earth'.

Then Maryland voted for gay marriage. Bob and Tracy were the first on Black Walnut Point to marry. Six other couples joined them, which got the attention of the Washington Post, television and international media outlets, which put them on the forefront of the revelation Tracy had received.

To celebrate their marriage, Tracy's father and family came to the Inn, and Tracy was pushed into his ministry. Now, Tracy marries many of the couples that come to Black Walnut Point to celebrate love.

"Whatever you do, just get here," He said, which Tracy did, and he said yes. Then Tracy realized the revelation of Peter, and that He is the Christ, the Son of the Living God. Now, Tracy continues demonstrating the 'love walk' to everyone who asks how he arrived. There, Tracy lives in his dreams, sees rainbows often - prisms of light through water - and he walks on those promises, walking on sunshine.

Selah

John 3:

² Beloved, I wish above all things
that thou mayest prosper and be in health,
even as thy soul prospereth.
³ For I rejoiced greatly,
when the brethren came
and testified of the truth that is in thee,
even as thou walkest in the truth.
⁴ I have no greater joy
than to hear that my children walk in truth.

ABOUT THE AUTHORS

Tracy met Bob in November of 2006. Nine months later, they were led to the end of Tilghman Island for the rendezvous planned for Tracy when he was three years old. Then, over the next three years, Bob learned about Tracy's life and his relationship with the Tall Shiny Silver Figure. During this time Bob had humorous articles published, wrote a few 'rehearsal books', and drafted chapters of Tracy's story. In June of 2010, Bob and Tracy became the Innkeepers of Black Walnut Point Inn, and the real adventure began. Tracy and Bob began revitalizing the Inn, and two years later the couple was married legally.

Aside from running the bed and breakfast, Bob and Tracy knew their actual job was telling the story of how they got to live in such a heavenly place in the middle of the Chesapeake Bay. This was an unusual question, as neither Bob nor Tracy had any previous thought of running an Inn, and had no experience doing so. Tracy had also grown up in West Virginia, Bob had grown up in Maine, and neither had ever been to the Bay side of the Eastern Shore of Maryland. However, if anyone asked, even if they happened to drive to the end of the road (as often happens on the point), their job was to tell the story of how they got there.

Seven years later, Bob and Tracy seriously set about writing the story down. Starting when Tracy first met the Tall Shiny Silver Figure when He showed Tracy the picture book of his life, the story took on a life of its own. As Bob took notes, organized, and interpreted Tracy's life experiences; more memories, lessons, and truths were revealed. Because the story of Tracy's relationship with the Tall Shiny Silver Figure bridged forty years, the scope of the book grew, as did the characters and anecdotes. The result is Dual Citizen, which is divided into three books: The Connection, The Training, and The Arrival. The trilogy captures the humor, sorrow, and eventual triumph Tracy experienced in reaching the all-important page of the picture book he was shone when he was three, which vantage point looked from the end of the dock at Black Walnut Point Inn.

By design, the story of Tracy and his relationship with the Tall Shiny Silver Figure prompts questions, and a need for more clarification than the books can hold within their pages. So Tracy and Bob also started the podcast of Dual Citizen. It contains introductions to each chapter by Tracy, and the audio book is read by Bob. Try it out, and if you like it, please tell someone about it and join the conversation: <u>Dual Citizen - The Podcast</u>.

60405174R00099

Made in the USA
Middletown, DE
15 August 2019